WILLIAM TREVOR

WILLIAM TREVOR

A study of his fiction

GREGORY A. SCHIRMER

ROUTLEDGE

LONDON AND NEW YORK

First published 1990
by Routledge
11 New Fetter Lane, London EC4P 4EE

Simultaneously published in the USA and Canada
by Routledge
a division of Routledge, Chapman and Hall, Inc.
29 West 35th Street, New York, NY 10001

Printed in Great Britain by
T J Press (Padstow) Ltd, Padstow, Cornwall

British Library Cataloguing in Publication Data

Schirmer, Gregory A.
William Trevor : a study of his fiction.
1. Fiction in English, 1945–   . Trevor, William,
1928–
I. Title
823'.914

ISBN 0-415-04493-6

Library of Congress Cataloging in Publication Data

Schirmer, Gregory A.
William Trevor: a study of his fiction / Gregory A. Schirmer.
p. cm.
Includes bibliographical references.
ISBN 0-415-04493-6
1. Trevor, William, 1928–   – Criticism and interpretation.
I. Title.
PR6070.R4Z87   1990   89–10914
823'.914–dc20

For Jane

CONTENTS

ACKNOWLEDGEMENTS

The author and publishers would like to extend their grateful thanks to the Bodley Head, and the Viking Penguin Corporation (USA) for permission to quote from the following: *The Old Boys, The Boarding House, Mrs Eckdorff in O'Neill's Hotel, Elizabeth Alone, The Children of Dynmouth, Other People's Worlds, The Day We Got Drunk on Cake, Angels at the Ritz, Fools of Fortune*, and, *The Silence in the Garden*.

"ONLY CONNECT":
Introduction

In 1910, the year Virginia Woolf chose as the birthdate of the modern sensibility, E. M. Forster published his penultimate novel, *Howards End*, a book that carried on its title page the phrase "Only Connect," and that expressed throughout Forster's belief in the need for compassion and connection, for a willingness to transcend lines of class, economics, and cultural taste in a society that seemed to Forster to be splintering into dangerously disparate groups. A dozen years and one world war later, that trust in the efficacy of an essentially humanistic moral vision seemed, to many, bleakly irrelevant; in 1922, T. S. Eliot's *The Wasteland* appeared in the pages of *Criterion* magazine, and its attitude toward Forster's principle of "Only Connect" could not have been plainer. "On Margate Sands," Eliot wrote, "I can connect/nothing with nothing."[1]

These two positions have served as starting points for much modern and post-modern literature. For William Trevor, an Anglo-Irishman whose eleven novels and six collections of short stories have earned him a respected position in contemporary English and Irish letters,[2] the tension between Forster's "Only Connect" and Eliot's "I can connect/nothing with nothing" has provided the governing moral force of his work. And although Trevor's writing is frequently admired – and rightly so – for its precision of style, its sensitivity to nuance of character and setting, and its subtle sense of comic irony, Trevor has always worked inside the mainstream tradition of fiction written out of strong moral commitments, and it is ultimately the moral dimension of his work, the complex vision of contemporary life generated by both an advocacy of Forster's principle of compassion and connection and a counterpointing, realistic assessment of contemporary society as alienated and disconnected, that makes him a writer of considerable significance, on both sides of the Irish Sea and on both sides of the Atlantic.

When Trevor's work first started attracting the notice of reviewers, in the middle and late 1960s, he was usually labelled a satirist or black humorist, and seen as principally preoccupied with the underside of contemporary British society; his fiction was frequently compared to that of Evelyn Waugh, Kingsley Amis, Graham Greene, Muriel Spark, and Ivy Compton-Burnett. This view of Trevor as chiefly a chronicler of losers, an ironist working out of a vision of despair, has unfortunately tended to stick.[3] It is, however, far too reductive to account for either the range of subject-matter in Trevor's writing or the breadth and complexity of his moral vision. Trevor has, for example, written at least as much about middle-class life in prosperous London suburbs as about lonely, alienated men and women wasting away in London bed-sitters or provincial Irish towns. He has written extensively about love and marriage, especially among the middle class, and some of his best work has to do with women and the elderly from various strata of society. His work encompasses both Irish and English life, and within the Irish tradition, he has written with equal authority about Protestant Ireland and Catholic Ireland. And he has frequently written out of a commitment to address some of the most pressing political and social issues of his day, especially in his native Ireland.

Trevor's ever-present irony also needs to be read not simply as an instrument for registering hopelessness and despair, but as a means of negotiating between Forster's "Only Connect" and Eliot's "I can connect/nothing with nothing," between an affirmation of the need for compassion and connection in contemporary society and a qualifying recognition of the full strength of the forces ranged against those values. This kind of irony requires distance, and much of the distance in Trevor's work is generated by his commitment to writing outside his own experience. "Personally," Trevor once said, "I . . . disagree with that awful advice that's always given to children: 'Write about what you know.' I'd say the opposite, in a way: 'You mustn't write about what you know. You must use your imagination.'"[4] Trevor has written short stories that draw on his youth in provincial Ireland,

and there are stories and parts of novels that owe something to his days in boarding-schools; but on the whole, very few traces of autobiography can be found in Trevor's fiction. It is no accident, for example, that his second and third novels, written when he was in his thirties, take as their principal focus the elderly. Nor is it an accident that Trevor has written more intimately about women than about men, nor that a number of his novels, like those of Dickens, rely on large canvasses with many characters from various walks of life. Trevor is, in fact, an admirer of Dickens, and even his view of Joyce, another strong influence on his work, reflects this bias; in Trevor's view, Joyce's greatest work, *Ulysses* – as distinct from the heavily autobiographical *A Portrait of the Artist as a Young Man* – stands squarely in the tradition of Dickens. "He worked very like Dickens," Trevor said in an interview. "He used lots and lots of acquaintances and turned them into characters in the book, but again like Dickens, he wrote at a distance."[5]

In somewhat the manner of Joyce, Trevor also has deliberately written at a geographical distance. Having left Ireland for England as a young man, Trevor wrote his early novels and stories almost exclusively about the least familiar of the two countries he knew – England. What Trevor said once about Elizabeth Bowen, another twentieth-century Anglo-Irish writer who devoted the larger part of her energies to writing about her adopted as opposed to her native country, describes equally well Trevor's own position as an Irishman writing about England: "She came to know England well, but always wrote about the English from an angle which suggests a stranger on the edge of a circle of friends."[6] In recent years, Trevor has increasingly written about Ireland, but only after he has become something of a stranger to it.

Not only has Trevor almost always written from this angle of exile, but also his life has been that of someone on the edge, of a spectator on the outside looking in. Born William Trevor Cox, in Mitchelstown, Co. Cork, Trevor had a childhood that was mobile to say the least. His father, James William Cox, was a bank official and the family moved frequently because of his work. Trevor once said that as a child he lived "like a middle-class gypsy" and: "We were always on the move. I found it impossible to make and keep friends because we were never in a single place for long enough. I have no roots."[7] Between the time he started going to school and the time he entered Trinity College, Dublin,

Trevor attended thirteen different schools, in provincial towns such as Skibbereen, Tipperary, Enniscorthy, Wexford, and Youghal. Moreover, a number of these schools were Catholic, and Trevor's family was Protestant. Trevor has written about the vagaries and varieties of his early education in his partly autobiographical collection of essays, *Old School Ties*:

> I attended many schools and for long periods of my childhood I attended no school at all, wandering the streets of provincial Irish towns untaught for months on end. Sometimes my brother and I were placed under the tutelage of a failed Christian Brother or a farmer's daughter who had passed the Intermediate Certificate Examination and would agree to come daily to the house. My mother found such figures in the same way as she found her endless string of maids, by driving out into the countryside and knocking on farmhouse doors.[8]

The frequent moving from one provincial town to another stopped in 1941, when Trevor, at the age of thirteen, enrolled at Sandford Park School in Dublin. From there he went to St Columba's College, also in Dublin, in 1943, and then to Trinity College. He took his degree, in history, from Trinity in 1950, and then spent a year in Dublin and two years in Armagh, Northern Ireland, teaching at a school before moving to England. Trevor taught art in the Midlands of England from 1953 to 1955, and then moved to southwest England, where he devoted himself to sculpting, eventually earning a small reputation as a sculptor.[9] In these years he also began writing, publishing his first novel, *A Standard of Behaviour*, in 1958. His second novel, *The Old Boys*, appeared in 1964, to considerable critical acclaim; a year later, he gave up a job in advertising that he had taken in 1960 to support his writing, and has since devoted himself fulltime to writing. He has continued to live in England, in the Devon countryside, with his wife Jane, whom he married in 1952. In recent years, he has divided his time between England, Ireland, and Italy, and, characteristically, has begun publishing some short stories with Italian settings. As he suggested in a recent interview, Trevor now finds himself in the position of feeling something of a stranger – the position he considers most advantageous for his writing – in several countries:

The country [Ireland] did not fall into place until I'd been in exile. Things you take for granted you don't actually see when you're living there. Every minute in Florence, for instance, you have to come to terms with something strange. It's a strangeness I still feel in England. I'm still puzzled and curious here.[10]

Trevor's tendency to court this feeling of strangeness, and to write about something only when he considers himself at a sufficient remove from it, has produced a body of writing extraordinarily broad in its range of interests. *A Standard of Behaviour* is set for the most part in Bohemian London, a reckless world of young, would-be artists and their circles of friends. This book may well contain some autobiographical elements drawn from Trevor's early years in England, when he was working to develop his writing and his sculpting, but this is an uncharacteristic novel, one which, moreover, Trevor has apparently tried to put behind him by regularly excluding it from lists of his published works. It is with *The Old Boys*, his second novel, that Trevor finds the style and voice – particularly the precise, understated note of irony – that have become his trademarks. It is also with this book, not coincidentally, that Trevor begins writing outside his own experience. Having to do with various intrigues among a group of old boys from an English public school, this novel, which won the Hawthornden Prize for Literature in 1964, also evidences a sharp sense of satire, and so inspired reviewers to draw comparisons between Trevor and writers like Waugh and Amis. *The Boarding-House*, Trevor's next novel, published in 1965, is markedly Dickensian in its scope and diversity of character. Set in a slightly seedy suburban boarding-house, this novel also carries Trevor into fictional territory that he has made his own, the shabby underside of society, populated by petty criminals and con-artists, lonely single men and women, sexually deviant or inadequate characters – people, in general, whom love and compassion have passed by. Along with *The Old Boys*, *The Boarding-House* established Trevor as an urban writer, and in his fourth novel, *The Love Department* (1966), he continued to write about London, but this time with a sharply different focus. This novel marks the beginning of Trevor's interest in writing about the suburban middle class, and about love and marriage. Although it is as much a moral fable as a realistic novel, *The Love Department* explores the marriages and affairs of its middle-class couples with pyschological authenticity. For Trevor, as this novel reveals, love and marriage are important barometers of human behavior, and his view of contemporary society as characterized by alienation and disconnection finds no more powerful objective correlative throughout his work than that of broken marriage and failed love.[11]

As their titles indicate, Trevor's three middle novels – *Mrs Eckdorf in O'Neill's Hotel* (1969), *Miss Gomez and the Brethren* (1971), and *Elizabeth Alone* (1973) – are written primarily from a woman's point of view. They are also, to one degree or another, concerned with love and marriage. But these books dramatize more pointedly than do the earlier novels the tension between a humanistic faith in the principle of compassion and connection and an ironic, qualifying view of contemporary society as alienated and disconnected. The central protagonist of *Mrs Eckdorf in O'Neill's Hotel*, a photo-journalist on the run from two failed marriages who arrives in Dublin to investigate the supposedly scandalous past of a rundown hotel, brings to her work an obsessive vision of man's moral responsibility to his fellow man. In the end, however, the sordid world that Mrs Eckdorf tries to save – a world in which human relationships are seen not as matters of love or selfless connection but as vehicles of exploitation or deceit – overwhelms her; her moral views are ignored and she herself ends in madness. *Miss Gomez and the Brethren* follows somewhat the same pattern, but is an even bleaker novel. Set in an urban-renewal area of London, a wasteland that reflects perfectly the moral barrenness of most of its characters, this book tracks the failures and failings of a protagonist considerably more alienated than Mrs Eckdorf – a Jamaican and an orphan who comes to London as a young woman only to find herself an outcast because of her class, race, and gender. Like Mrs Eckdorf, Miss Gomez is inspired by a moral vision of man's need for connection and compassion, but also like Mrs Eckdorf, Miss Gomez finds no one to listen to her. *Elizabeth Alone*, Trevor's seventh novel, is one of his most ambitious – it is a large book, with an extensive cast of characters embracing everything from the suburbs of the upper-middle classes to seedy city neighborhoods worked by con-artists and petty criminals – and certainly the most successful in terms of his efforts to write from a woman's point of view and about love and marriage. It is also a more affirmative novel than the two books that precede it;

its protagonist, a well-to-do suburban widow, does come to understand – mainly through a series of relationships that brings her into contact with people from different classes and cultural backgrounds – the importance of compassion, and the book ends with more than a fleeting suggestion of her prospects for a sounder, healthier life.

Trevor has said that he is not a political writer – except in so far as his work is, in his words, "based on an objection to the intolerances and conventions that . . . society has generated"[12] – but in his two later novels, *The Children of Dynmouth* (1976) and *Other People's Worlds* (1980), Trevor's view of the contemporary world as alienated and disconnected is manifested to a considerable degree in a depiction of the inherent moral wrongs of the class system. Timothy Gedge, the 15 year-old protagonist of *The Children of Dynmouth* (which won the Whitbread Literary Award in 1976), is portrayed pointedly as a victim of the class system, someone locked into a life of working-class drudgery and alienation from which there seems to be no escape. Unlike Pinkie in Graham Greene's *Brighton Rock* – and the comparison seems appropriate in part because *The Children of Dynmouth* is set in an English seaside town – Timothy is less an embodiment of evil as defined by a religious point of view than a victim of a society that has abandoned Forster's humanistic principle of connection. In *Other People's Worlds*, the ill-advised marriage of Julia Ferndale, a genteel woman used to a life of social privilege and bucolic tranquillity, to a man who turns out to be one of Trevor's most pathetic and sinister con-artists, plunges her into an unsettling but ultimately morally enlightening confrontation with an entire world of urban, lower-class life defined by chaos and despair.

Many of the formal qualities of Trevor's novels, including their frequent use of juxtaposition and parallelism, are particularly suited to the short story, and Trevor's work in this genre can hardly be overestimated. Falling somewhere between the radical experimentalism of high modernist writers and the more or less traditional methods of the realistic short story, Trevor's stories depend heavily on suggestion, irony, and cinematic juxtaposition. In thematic terms, they tend to be relatively bleak; characters in them rarely discover the means to overcome their feelings of alienation or the crippling illusions that they rely on to mask their inadequacies, and so there is little promise of moral redemption.

7

Among the most effective of Trevor's stories in this vein are those
that use the corruption or destruction of love – marriages ending
in divorce or separation, love replaced by casual sexual relationships, romance worn down by time and circumstance – as an
objective correlative. In Trevor's three latest collections, however
– *Lovers of Their Time* (1978), *Beyond the Pale* (1981), and *The News
from Ireland* (1986) – his stories have increasingly been informed by
political and social concerns, portraying characters caught in con-
flicts between private values such as love and family loyalties and
the impersonal forces of history or political ideology.

Not surprisingly, some of the most powerful of Trevor's writing
of this kind has to do, directly or indirectly, with the sectarian
violence in contemporary Northern Ireland. Seamus Heaney once
said that the literary artist confronted with political catastrophe
must "deal with public crisis by making your own terrain take the
color of it,"[13] and Trevor's fiction about the Ulster conflict places
the violence and divisiveness squarely in the context of the broad
moral vision that informs most of his work. His short stories
having to do with Ulster tend to see the political and religious
fanaticism that has fuelled much of the violence there as a product
of the abandonment of humanistic values, but they also often see
the conflict as an experience that forces individuals into taking
moral stands inspired by a humanistic belief in connection, into
recognizing a moral obligation that extends, often at considerable
cost to the individual, beyond private concerns and needs. This
complex moral vision also informs Trevor's two most recent, and
most insistently historical, novels, *Fools of Fortune* (which won the
Whitbread Prize for Fiction in 1983) and *The Silence in the Garden*
(1988). The central relationship in *Fools of Fortune*, between the son
of an Anglo-Irish Protestant landowning family and his distant
English cousin, is played out against a violent backdrop of
historical and political events that eventually, and with tragic
inevitability, destroy their love. At the same time, the novel also
applauds the individual's willingness to act, at whatever cost to
private needs and desires, in a way that recognizes a moral obligation larger than that to one other human being. The principal
focus of *The Silence in the Garden* is the demise in the early decades
of this century of a once prosperous Anglo-Irish Protestant family.
But this subject-matter, despite its echoes of Yeats, is specifically
in the service of Trevor's concern with the conflict between

individual values and political ideology and fanaticism. This is a thoroughly tragic novel, one in which most of the characters are crushed under the unavoidable weight brought to bear on their lives by Ireland's long, violent past – "*a thread of carnage,*" as one character puts it, "*that was unbearable even to think about,*"[14] and one that is still tragically visible in today's Northern Ireland.

Trevor has described himself as "the least experimental of writers,"[15] and he is working in a tradition that is arguably less given to experimentalism than is that of American or continental fiction. But British (and Irish) writing is more conscious of modernist and post-modernist departures from convention than is often assumed, and Trevor has absorbed into his essentially traditional fiction a number of techniques usually associated with modernist fiction and its various offspring. In large part, these techniques have in common a distrust of narrative omniscience, and so are crucial to the expression of Trevor's moral vision – one that constantly needs to qualify even its most tentative affirmations of compassion and connection with the recognition that the contemporary world is hostile ground for such values.[16]

The most striking of these narrative strategies is the use of multiple centers of consciousness. Trevor's fiction tends to be constructed of many segments, each of which is associated with one character, or dominated by one character's perception. The result is a mosaic of different points of view, relying heavily on juxtaposition and parallelism. This technique is hardly new to the twentieth century – Dickens used it frequently – but Trevor is inheriting it less from Dickens than from modernist writers like Conrad, James, Woolf, and Joyce, for whom limited points of view embodied in formal terms a philosophical scepticism. More specifically, Trevor uses multiple centers of consciousness to shift back and forth between an interior view of a character and various exterior views, and therefore to negotiate between sympathy and irony, intimacy and distance, and, in larger terms, affirmation and qualfication. At the same time, fictions constructed out of such fragments present narrative fabrics that themselves embody the idea of connection; Trevor's novels and stories are essentially networks of perceptions and attitudes, and the reader is forced to make connections between the various points – to enact, in the process of reading, the principle of connection.

The other technique that Trevor relies on consistently to create ironic, qualifying pressure in his fiction is the manipulation of narrative voice. Trevor's writing has more often than not been described as dominated by a cool, distant, largely unjudging narrative tone. In fact, narrators of this stripe appear in pure form only occasionally in Trevor's work; the bulk of Trevor's narration is strongly colored by individual characters, usually the center of consciousness in a given passage. This strategy enables Trevor to avoid, if not actually undermine, narrative omniscience at the same time that it enhances the effect of his use of multiple centers of consciousness. In this kind of fiction, characters tend to be defined by their own subjectivity, often embodied in the narrative voice that controls the sections in which they are the center of consciousness; by the views of other characters, revealed in part through the narrative voice that controls *their* sections; and, on occasion, by a relatively neutral narrator who sees things from a distant, supposedly objective point of view. This flexible narrative voice thereby helps establish and maintain those complex balances between interior and exterior views of characters – and thus between sympathy and irony, intimacy and distance – that are so crucial to the vision that informs Trevor's writing.

Given this use of multiple centers of consciousness and of a narrative voice that takes its tone from different characters, juxtaposition and parallelism are obviously important to Trevor's fiction. One of the most dramatic forms of juxtaposition that Trevor employs is that between an extremely intimate point of view and a distant, birds-eye point of view. These shifts from passages in which the narrative voice is closely identified with a given character to essentially panoramic perspectives – a technique that owes something to Virginia Woolf (especially *Mrs Dalloway*) and something to James Joyce (especially the "Wandering Rocks" episode of *Ulysses*) – generate precisely the kind of ironic qualification that Trevor is almost always working for; the force of individual passions or attitudes is inevitably defused or undercut when seen from a perspective in which the individual appears relatively insignificant.

Trevor is not a metafictional writer. There are, however, a number of characters in his novels and stories who clearly are authorial figures. Not surprisingly, these characters tend to be driven by strong moral instincts, in some instances by an almost missionary-like zeal to make other people see the truth of their lives. Trevor is, after all, working in the mainstream of British fiction, and, as one critic of the British novel has put it, that genre "has always believed that the most important issues are moral issues, and that moral issues, whilst they may be difficult, are ultimately tractable."[17] And yet, however tractable the issues may ultimately be, the authorial surrogates in Trevor's writing almost always fail in their ambition to act as moral agents. This, too, reflects Trevor's vision of both contemporary society and the contemporary artist. In his short story "Beyond the Pale," a middle-aged Englishwoman named Cynthia, suddenly caught up in the terrorism of contemporary Irish politics, tries to make her English travelling companions, on holiday in Northern Ireland, see their connection to the destructive realities lying just beyond the false harbor of their seaside inn. Like so many of Trevor's authorial characters, Cynthia finds that her story, and its moral implications, are soundly ignored. And yet she believes, as does Trevor, that the truth must be told, that there is always the chance that it might make a difference. "No one cares," Cynthia tells herself after her tale has been told. "No one cares, and on our journey home we shall all four be silent. Yet is the truth about ourselves at least a beginning?"[18]

2

"A FARCE IN A VALE OF TEARS":
The Early Novels

Trevor's first published novel, *A Standard of Behaviour* (1958), opens with this passage:

> On the last but one of my schooldays the Headmaster, a man I remember, greatly put about by women, both his wife and daughter being morally unreliable in the company of men, presented me with a small red volume, containing, it was said, the sayings and doings of the saint after whom the school was named and to whom it was in some way vaguely dedicated. If the giving was accompanied by words they are now forgotten, as indeed are many of the utterances of this good man, which I believe is what he was, although at the time the fact did not always register with us.[1]

Trevor's next novel, *The Old Boys*, published six years later, begins as follows:

> The meeting was late in starting because Mr Turtle had trouble with the lift. Having arrived successfully at Gladstone House, he entered the lift, struck the button marked 5 and ascended. On the way he began to think, and his train of thought led him into the past and absorbed him. At the fifth floor Mr Turtle still thought; and when the lift was summoned from below he descended with it. A man in overalls opened the doors at the basement and Mr Turtle got out. 'Thank you, thank you,' he said to the man. 'Room three-o-five,' he said to himself; but all he could find was an enormous lavatory and a furnace-room. The concrete passages did not seem right to Mr Turtle, nor did the gloomy green and cream walls, the bare electric light bulbs

and the smell of Jeyes' Fluid. 'I say,' Mr Turtle said to a woman who was mopping the floor, 'can you tell me where three-o-five is?' The woman didn't hear him. He repeated the question and she stared at him with suspicion.

'Three-o-five? Do you want Mr Morgan?'

'I think I'm a little lost actually. Actually I want room three-o-five.' The woman didn't know what Mr Turtle meant by room three-o-five. Her province was the basement.

'I'm sorry,' she said, mopping round Mr Turtle's feet. 'I don't know no room three-o-five.'

'I'll be late. I'm due at a meeting.'

'They didn't tell me about no meeting. You won't find no meeting in the basement, mister.'

Mr Turtle registered surprise.

'Is this the basement?'[2]

The differences between these two passages are striking. The first, with its self-conscious verbosity and convoluted syntax – as well as the stock situation of a first-person narrator looking back on his schooldays – might have come from the hand of any novice English writer in the 1950s. The second, in addition to being more direct and finely honed in matters of diction and sentence structure, is quite distinctive: the eccentricity of character and situation (Mr Turtle seems to have materialized directly from the pages of a Dickens novel), the reserved, neutral voice of the third-person narrator, and the just-perceptible ironic tilt administered to the entire passage by certain slightly skewed words and phrases ("*struck* the button," "ascended," "Her *province* was the basement") all mark the passage as Trevor's.

Trevor obviously found his voice early; setting aside *A Standard of Behaviour* (often dropped from lists of Trevor's published work), Trevor's early novels are remarkably confident and accomplished pieces of writing. They are by no means unflawed – *The Old Boys* is at times too self-consciously shaped by formal considerations, *The Boarding-House* courts eccentricity a bit too eagerly, and *The Love Department* wobbles rather unsteadily between realism and romance – but on the whole they show surprisingly few signs of being the work of an apprentice. Moreover, many of the formal techniques that characterize Trevor's mature work, and many of his most pervasive thematic preoccupations, are to be found in them. It is in these books, for example, that Trevor begins experimenting with multiple centers of consciousness, panoramic perspectives, and the archly stylized prose observable in the passage describing Mr Turtle – all techniques crucial to the ironic perspective that shapes the world of Trevor's fiction. And it is in these novels that the distinctly moral dimensions of that world first emerge, specifically the need for compassion and connection in a society governed by alienation and disconnection.

Trevor's interests in these three novels, with the partial exception of *The Love Department*, seem curiously out of the way; the election of a president to an old boys association, the day-to-day life of a suburban boarding-house full of doddering, Dickensian residents, the "love department" of a popular magazine run by a demented, gnome-like reincarnation of Miss Lonelyhearts. Reviewers were quick to classify these books as satire, black humor, comedy of manners; Dickens was usually mentioned, and the more contemporary names of Evelyn Waugh, Kingsley Amis, Graham Greene, Muriel Spark, and Ivy Compton-Burnett were invoked.[3] But these early evaluations tended to overlook or undervalue the moral and psychological depths that, at times, these novels achieved. Their eccentric, crowded surfaces may be satiric or comic, but their ironies often have tragic implications. The world that they present is very like that a character in *The Love Department* says he found when he ventured forth into the world from the confines of a monastery: "A farce in a vale of tears."[4]

A STANDARD OF BEHAVIOUR

The least characteristic and least successful of Trevor's eleven published novels, *A Standard of Behaviour* nevertheless merits some attention, if only to show how much ground Trevor gained in moving from it to *The Old Boys*. The highly mannered, transparently imitative style (Anthony Powell seems the most obvious model), the reflective first-person narrator, a plot that turns on a young man searching for meaning in a bewildering, meaningless universe – all these Trevor was to jettison when he came to write *The Old Boys*. Also, the novel's vision of contemporary life, embodied in the collapse of the narrator's faith in "a certain standard of reasonably intelligent behaviour" (p. 102) in the face of a world that seems to render that standard irrelevant, is radically redefined and refined by the time Trevor gets to *The Old Boys*.

A flaw in the book's basic structure most clearly reveals it to be the work of a novice. In the first third of the book, the first-person narrator is much less important than that which he describes; like the third-person narrators in later Trevor novels, he functions chiefly as a window onto a relatively large cast of comic characters, a collection of Bohemian ne'er-do-wells that might have stepped out of an early Evelyn Waugh novel: Nigel Townsend, a would-be painter but actual con-artist (a precursor of later Trevor characters like Septimus Tuam in *The Love Department* and Francis Tyte in *Other People's Worlds*); Otto Hasenfuss, a wealthy young German playing the stock part of the bewildered and easily swindled foreigner; Edmund Archer, an obscure, silent farmer who harbors a secret, and woefully misguided, ambition to be a poet; David Aldridge, a laconic young sculptor whose one exhibition, financed by Otto, achieves renown only after it is the target of an arranged break-in; Mrs Lamont and her two sensual daughters, operators of the narrator's boarding-house, and sponsors of a nudist party filled with "bright young things"; and Virginia de Whitt, a beautiful but aimless young woman whom the narrator falls in love with at first sight and then loses when she decides, on an apparent whim, to marry Archer.

But once the narrator meets Virginia, about a third of the way through the book, the focus shifts away from Townsend and his eccentric associates and toward the narrator and his psychological state. Moreover, the comedy and satire that dominate the first part of the novel suddenly give way to a story of loss and dissolution: the narrator loses Virginia to Archer; Archer kills himself, presumably in despair over his failure to publish his poems; Aldridge rapes the woman he thinks he is in love with, then marries someone else; Otto returns to Germany, scared off by anonymous threatening letters written by Nigel as a way of getting Otto out of the way before he can discover how badly Nigel has defrauded him; and Nigel himself wanders off to France, to be seen only one more time by the narrator.

The first part of the book has not, however, prepared the ground for this change. For one thing, the character of the narrator is far too thin to bear the weight of being the central figure, or to provide the psychological authenticity called for. Moreover, the other characters are not easily converted from their earlier roles as clowns and eccentrics to the more taxing parts of reflectors for the narrator's character; some are too one-dimensional (Nigel, Mrs Lamont, Otto) and others too vague (Virginia, Archer, Aldridge) to shed much light on the inner life of the narrator. The narrator's thoughts about other characters, therefore, tend to be relatively meaningless, as in this reflection, prompted by a remark from a clergyman, J. R. Pollack, who is mischievously invited to Mrs Lamont's nudist party:

> In an odd way, for he was not a person I thought at all about, I was immediately reminded of Archer. The character of Mr Pollack and that of Archer had, superficially, hardly anything in common; yet this remark about the value of a convivial evening was, I guessed, precisely the one Archer would have made. Whether or not Mr Pollack had 'got somewhere' during the evening; whether or not it had advanced him in his vocation, I did not know. The same doubt would have applied in Archer's case; assuming, that is, that his vocation was, as he seemed to insist it to be, that of a poet. Yet in spite of not quite knowing what the word 'value' connoted for either of them I felt sure that what Mr Pollack had derived from the party was of the same kind as Archer would have, had he been present.
>
> (p. 74)

Despite its tone of weighty consideration, the passage reveals next to nothing about the narrator, largely because neither Archer nor Mr Pollack has been defined fully enough for the reader to make any judgments about the narrator on the strength of his attitudes toward them.

For all its failings, *A Standard of Behaviour* does offer a few glimpses of the mature Trevor. The bleak underside of contemporary London, for example – realized so powerfully in *Miss Gomez and the Brethren* and *Other People's Worlds* – can be found tucked into odd corners of this early work, as in this description of Aldridge's flat in a rundown district of the city:

> We took our leave and began the journey between the attic room and the street. This, for me, owing to my great fear of cats, which now seemed to abound in excess, was fraught with

16

terrors. The flight of stairs from the attic to the next floor was rickety, unlighted and narrow. It was on this stretch of our itinerary that we came across the main body of these wretched animals, which were, Aldridge had told us, communal. Crouched by the numerous holes in the floorboards or crawling perilously along the bannister rail, they paused in their labours only to snarl alarmingly at us and stretch out their lean claws. The rest of the way was gloomy, with the light of the failing day filtering through dusty glass. Halfway down a dog fought lethargically with a small diseased kitten. A girl in a petticoat crossed the landing from one room to another, whistling sourly between her teeth. There was a smell of human dirt and ill-kept lavatories.

(pp. 28–9)

And there are passages in which the decided ironic tilt of Trevor's mature style is to be glimpsed: "It was also in Townsend's company that he [Aldridge] began to appear at the more select artistic or vaguely intellectual gatherings held from time to time by hostesses who were anxious, more often than not, to atone for their husbands' fiscal connection with the scrap-iron, bone, or fish trades" (p. 49); and "my mother ended a rambling and, to judge by the illegible condition of the content, tearful account of her own married life with the injunction that I must, before pledging myself, be satisfied that: *the girl is not a Methodist*" (p. 87).

None the less, it is only with the appearance on the first page of *The Old Boys* of the likeably inept Mr Turtle, striking that lift button and descending to the green and cream walls and the smell of Jeyes' Fluid in the basement, that the reader finds himself in the new and distinctive fictional territory that Trevor was quickly to make his own.

THE OLD BOYS

It is with *The Old Boys* that Trevor emerges as a comic writer of significant stature. This novel, ostensibly concerned with the efforts of the elderly Mr Jaraby to secure his election as president of an Old Boys Association, employs a wide variety of comic modes, from the relatively crude comedy of slapstick to the more sophisticated, subtle humor of puns and word-plays. If Dickens is one obvious forerunner, so, perhaps less obviously, is Samuel Beckett, whose influence is felt most clearly in the novel's dialogue.[5] This typical exchange between the Jarabys – occurring just after the death of Mr Turtle on Old Boys Day, the death of Mr Jaraby's cat, Monmouth, at the hands of Mrs Jaraby, and the return home of the Jarabys's deeply troubled son, Basil, along with his pet birds – is reminiscent of nothing so much as the conversations between such quarreling pairs as Didi and Gogo, Hamm and Clov, Mercier and Camier:

'Turtle died during *The Mikado*. They had to scrap the last act.'

'Your cat too,' cried Mrs Jaraby. 'Returned to his Maker. And Basil back in residence.'

'What residence? What do you say?'

'Basil is with us again. He is above us now, cages of birds festoon the house. Hark, and you may hear them.'

'Is Basil here? With birds?'

'Be calm a moment. Sit down, compose yourself. Ask me question by question. The answers required vary.'

'It is you who should compose yourself. You are going on in a mad way. What is all this?'

'I am breaking news to you; why don't you listen?'

'What of Monmouth? Is Monmouth injured?'

'Injured unto death. Does that mean dead? It doesn't, does it? You missed the monster's passing.'

'Is Monmouth dead?'

'I have said so with variation.'

'Monmouth and Turtle too. My God, my God!'

'He is not just your God. "Our God, our God!" should be your cry.' . . .

'You are mocking my sorrow. I am brought low by sudden deaths and you jest and jeer, since you are made that way. Have you no word of comfort?'

'I have made practical suggestions. Act on them and you may find relief. As to pets, there are new pets now in the house; you need not feel cut off from the animal kingdom.'

'What pets are new? How can I understand if you speak in this way? You make no sense at all.'

'I speak only repetitively. I have already said there are eight new coloured birds in cages. They are bred as pets, bought and sold in millions.'

'Why is Basil here? If he has brought this circus with him, then he and it must go at once. I did not give any consent, I did not invite him.'

'Your son replaces your cat. You leave in the house an animal, you return to welcome a human form. It is almost a fairy story.'

(p. 129, pp. 131–2)

Despite the novel's comic surface – and despite the usual reading of it as a satire on English public schools and on the larger social system behind them[6] – *The Old Boys* is informed by an essentially bleak vision that is interested in serious moral issues. The division between the Jarabys, which anticipates Trevor's later interest in failed marriages, dramatizes the idea of disconnection on the private, intimate level of marriage. "All our conversations are ridiculous," Mrs Jaraby tells her husband late in the book. "We speak without communication" (p. 138). The theme is also worked out in the broken relationship between Mr Jaraby and his son. In the heat of a quarrel with his wife, Mr Jaraby suggests that Basil, after he first got into trouble, should have gone away and taken "a name that cut off all connection" (p. 171). Then, in the book's most dramatic moment, fearing that his son's arrest for child molestation might jeopardize his chances to be elected president of the Old Boys Association, Mr Jaraby denies his paternity. "He is not my son," he tells the astonished association members. "My wife's only. By a previous marriage" (p. 185).

Mrs Jaraby's efforts to restore Basil to what she sees as his rightful place in the family, although a source for much of the comic interplay between the Jarabys, spring from a deeply rooted loneliness, something that most of Trevor's characters experience at one time or another. In one of the novel's rare interior monologues, Mrs Jaraby fantasizes about Basil's coming to live with them, revealing, with hardly a trace of the novel's usual comic irony, her fears of loneliness and her desperate need for some kind of human connection:

I shall wake in the mornings and hear the sound of birds, and take an interest in them and go with him to shows. People shall come to the house to see them and buy them, not people who are old and lonely and of uncertain temper, but men who talk enthusiastically of their interest, who can tell the quality of a bird and can talk about it, so that one may learn in time to tell it too, and exchange a point of view.

(p. 83)

Even minor characters whose roles seem essentially comic often advance this darker side of the novel. Mr Sole's and Mr Cridley's attempts to increase the amount of correspondence that they receive by soliciting junk-mail are both comic and pathetic, and no character in the novel expresses the idea of alienation with more conviction than does Mr Turtle. Indeed, the development of Mr Turtle from a flat figure of pure farce in the early parts of the novel to a sympathetic embodiment of the feelings of loss associated with old age is one of the reasons that this novel cannot be described adequately as a satire or a comedy of manners.

Mr Turtle's characterization is accomplished largely by careful modulations between comic surfaces and psychological depths that demand sympathy. The opening scene, for example, in which Mr Turtle winds up lost and bewildered in the basement, is replayed later through his consciousness, forcing an introspective, empathic revision of the situation:

> Mr Turtle was ashamed of himself. He was ashamed that he could make no hand of the loneliness that had crept upon him. He was ashamed that he could let his mind wander so, and watch it wander and not care; that he had to ask so often for words to be repeated to him, and had invented a story that he was deaf. When the committee had last met, for instance, it had seemed to Mr Turtle that the men around the table were not at all what they were but Ponders major, Sole, Cridley, Jaraby, Swabey-Boyns, Nox, Sanctuary: the boys they had been, sitting thus to arrange a rugger team or talk some inter-House business. To Mr Turtle they seemed fresh-faced and young, starting out on a life that he had finished with; patiently and kindly waiting for him to find his way from the basement to the room, and not blaming him at all, because they accepted that he should make mistakes.
>
> (p. 42)

These kinds of reflective speculations pave the way for the chapter devoted exclusively to Mr Turtle's wanderings through the school grounds on Old Boys Day, the day of his death. In this chapter, the same shifts between surface action and introspective review deepen Mr Turtle's character, build sympathy for him, and strengthen his symbolic function as an embodiment of loneliness and alienation; jests among the old boys at the dinner table about Mr Turtle's feelings for Miss Burdock, for example, are interiorized later: "Why should they interfere with his life like this? Why should they talk against Miss Burdock? What business was it of anyone's but his that he was getting married? Old men got married, no one prevented them. . . . Did they know what it was to be always escaping from the images in his mind, and seeking people to talk to in parks?" (p. 111).

An undercurrent of violence runs just beneath the surface of this novel, coming up in such moments as the beating of Nox when he was a schoolboy and the spectacular scene in which Mrs Jaraby drowns her husband's cat. Basil Jaraby is the primary agent of this dark force, and like other sinister figures in Trevor's novels, he is characterized with considerable psychological realism and a carefully controlled ambivalence of attitude. In the first part of the novel, Basil seems a harmless eccentric, a lonely, frustrated man inexplicably preoccupied with raising pet budgerigars. When Trevor is ready to disclose Basil's true criminality – he is, in fact, a child molester – he does so by replaying the moment of a specific crime through Basil's memory:

> As he stood in the centre of his room, his stomach twitching with anxiety, he remembered the purloining of the nail. He was thinking that he should have told the woman about it. He should have tried to explain to her that bringing her little girl to see his birds was another action of the same kind; that his life had been constructed of actions like that; that he meant no harm at all. And the little girl hadn't been frightened. She had done what he had asked her to do, and only afterwards – when he had led her back to the playground in the park, fearing that she might not know her way; when her mother had shouted at her and at him – only then had she said that she was afraid.
>
> (p. 126)

By forcing the reader so close to Basil's point of view, this passage, at the same time that it reveals the full horror of Basil's actions, inevitably generates sympathy for him and so implicitly raises questions about whether characters like Basil are more victims of a society that has abandoned the principle of compassion and connection than victimizers.

That principle, which later becomes so important to Trevor's view of contemporary society, is embodied in the formal structure of *The Old Boys*, specifically in its organization around multiple centers of consciousness. The novel is written from a number of different perspectives that are connected, ultimately, by the reader. This network of varying points of view also tends to generate that balance between sympathy and irony, intimacy and distance, assertion and qualification so crucial to Trevor's dramatization of a vision that both sees the need for compassion and connection, and has serious doubts as to their efficacy.

This structural pattern depends heavily for its effect on Trevor's handling of narrative voice. In any given scene, the voice of the narrator tends to be colored strongly by whatever character is functioning as the scene's center of consciousness. The diction, syntax, imagery, and rhythms of the passage quoted above describing Basil's thoughts differ radically from the qualities of this description of Mr Jaraby's worries about losing control of his household: "What of the house he owned and called his own? Must he accept that it was now an unreliable place, where anything could happen? The sitting-room and the garden, once havens of rest, were fearful places now; uneasy places, rich in defiance and chaos" (p. 151). A markedly different tone characterizes the narrative voice when it describes the feelings of another of the old boys, Mr Swabey-Boyns:

> Once he had been Boyns major of great repute; arrogant and powerful; swaggering, magnificent Boyns; Boyns in some trouble over a boy called Slocombe, accused of corrupting the boy and lying his way to safety. He had run into Slocombe five or six years ago, just before his death: beetle-browed, moustached, his face scrawny, the flesh seeming of some other substance, Slocombe who had been in his time the beauty of the Lower Fourth, Slocombe whose hand he had clutched on a walk, to whom he had later read the *Idylls of the King*.
>
> (pp. 180–1)

Despite the lyrical and generally sympathetic tone, complete sympathy for Mr Swabey-Boyns's romanticized memories of the past is prevented by the third-person point of view with its ever-present threat of ironic undercutting. Indeed, in all these passages, the distance afforded by third-person narration is closed to some extent by the narrator's adoption of the character's voice, but it is not eliminated altogether.

One other technique that Trevor employs, beginning with *The Old Boys*, to maintain ironic pressure on his material is what might be called panoramic perspectives, a device used by both Joyce and Woolf, often for similar purposes. A sudden pulling-back of the point of view to a remote, birds-eye position, this technique introduces ironic qualifications by forcing the specific characters and events of the novel into a large, deflating context of indifference. Trevor tends to apply this kind of perspective in the immediate wake of scenes of high emotional voltage, such as the heated arguments between the Jarabys. Perhaps the most effective use of the panoramic perspective in this novel occurs immediately after the climactic scene in which Mr Jaraby denies that Basil is his son:

> Rain came on the night of the committee meeting. It dripped from the garden gnomes in Crimea Road and lay in pools on the caked lawns. The sky was dark and bleak; dried leaves rattled on the suburban trees. In small back gardens children's toys lay scattered, their tired paint revived. Wallflowers and the last of the roses were fresh again in the gloom.
>
> The rain spread from the west. It fell in Somerset in late afternoon; it caught the evening crowds unprepared in London. A woman, glad to see it, walked through it in a summer dress. A man in Putney, airing his dog, lost his dog on the common and died in October of a cold that had become pneumonia. The umbrellas of the cautious, a handful only, moved smugly through Knightsbridge. Seagulls darted on the river; elderly tramps huddled around a tea-stall near Waterloo Bridge, talking of winter doss-houses. Women whose place was the streets stared at the rain morosely from windows in Soho, wondering how the change would affect their business and guessing the worst. People with rheumatism said it would affect their bones and recalled the pain that the damp air presaged.
>
> (p. 186)

In addition to defusing the denial scene, this passage, with its

23

Wasteland imagery, sounds the note of death and decay that runs through the entire book, and points to the bleak, even tragic ending of this novel that seems, at times, so essentially comic. Mr Jaraby is, in the end, not elected president, Basil is arrested, and Mrs Jaraby, a frustrated agent of compassion and connection, is left empty-handed, with only the old familiar routines to help pass the time, and ruminating in a most Beckettian fashion: "We are left to continue as we have continued; as the days fall by, to lose our faith in the advent of an early coffin" (p. 190). Her final words to her husband – and the novel's last words – carry an ironic charge that seems to close off any possibility of hope or redemption: "Come now, how shall we prove that we are not dead?" (p. 191).

THE BOARDING-HOUSE

The Old Boys, for all its considerable finesse, moves within relatively narrow social boundaries. *The Boarding-House*, published a year after *The Old Boys*, is, on the other hand, one of Trevor's baggiest, most Dickensian novels, and its large and varied cast of eccentrics and ne'er-do-wells cuts a relatively wide swath through English society. (Both novels, however, ignore the suburban middle class, taken up for the first time in *The Love Department*.) And although more than a few of the many characters in *The Boarding-House* threaten to degenerate into caricatures,[7] and their sheer number at times dissipates the book's narrative drive, the book has a human density and weight not always evident in the more tightly controlled *Old Boys*. Characterization, in some instances, is deeper and more complex, and the diverse cast of characters as a whole constitutes a powerful, multiple embodiment of loneliness and alienation. And finally, because the residents of William Bird's boarding-house, unlike the members of the relatively homogenous Old Boys Association, cross many social, sexual, and racial lines, *The Boarding-House* presents a more dramatic, more realistic frame for the working out of Trevor's faith in connection, or what he called in an interview, "that tiny area of 'getting together'":

I have a thing about different kinds of people being drawn together for what you would call mechanical reasons. . . . It's accidental, it's incidental, it's just a coincidence, and I like the idea of people who are very different having to work together, having to converse even, simply because they are in the same room. One of the things which I find very important and very absurd in life, very, very farcical, is the way you can take people of very different views and put them together and they don't get on at all; they quarrel. But, if you can slightly twist the situation, give it the novelist's turn, you make them get on very well. There is, in fact, always that tiny area of 'getting together'. Either you choose to use it or you choose to ignore it. Class divisions, colour divisions, sex divisions, they are all absurd.[8]

As frequently happens in Trevor's fiction, that vision of human connection is sharply qualified in *The Boarding-House* by an ironic undercurrent that makes itself felt in a number of ways. For one thing, the bonds between the various misfits and solitaries gathered in and around Mr Bird's boarding-house are tenuous; Mr Studdy, Trevor's first real con-man, has very little in common with Major Eele, an embittered elderly man whose failures with women have driven him to pornography, and even less with Mr Venables, whose one love-affair, years ago, produced a child and a life-long sense of crippling guilt, or Mr Scribbin, a painfully shy man in his late fifties inexplicably fond of recordings of train noises. Nurse Clock, whose name suggests the mechanical professionalism with which she masks her fears and aggressions, has almost nothing in common with Miss Clerricot, a middle-aged secretary whose acute loneliness kindles a pathetically romanticized interest in her boss, or Rose Cave, a spinster in her fifties who spent her first forty-one years living alone with her mother. The last quarter of the novel is devoted to the dismantling of this loosely knit community by the merciless and greedy Nurse Clock– Mr Studdy partnership, culminating in the final, physical destruction of the boarding-house at the hands of Tome Obd, the Nigerian resident driven mad by the disintegration of his illusory relationship with Annabel Tonks.

The bleakness of the novel's ending is underscored by several ironically panoramic perspectives applied in the closing pages. One of these widens the focus from the fire that destroys the boarding-house to several of the minor characters whose lives have touched, however briefly, some of the residents of the boarding-house:

> In Wimbledon Mrs Rush, who had been Janice Brownlow, slept and did not know, or ever know, about the fire in the boarding-house. Mrs Maylam knew because an hour or so later Studdy knocked on the door of her flat and asked for a couch to rest on. Mrs le Tor knew in time because she heard about it, and wondered until she was told to the contrary if Major Eele had perished. 'A black man died,' her informant said, and Mrs le Tor recalled that Major Eele had talked about African women but had not touched upon the African male. . . .
>
> Far away, in her flat at the top of the flights of stone stairs, Annabel Tonks slept and knew nothing of the fire. She stretched in her sleep and was aware of the luxury of the movement.[9]

This indifference is the final manifestation of the loneliness and disconnection that have haunted the boarding-house residents all through the book.

Ironic pressure is also exerted on almost every page of the novel by the same self-consciously stylized prose and dialogue found in *The Old Boys*. The opening of *The Boarding-House* provides an example of how the formal, even archaic diction and syntax of Trevor's narration hold the reader at a distance:

> 'I am dying,' said William Wagner Bird on the night of August 13th, turning his face towards the wall for privacy, sighing at the little bunches of forget-me-not on the wallpaper. He felt his body a burden in the bed, a thing he did not know. His feet seemed far away, and it came to him abruptly that he was aware of his feet in an intellectual way only. It passed through Mr Bird's mind then that physical communication with his nether half was forever gone.
>
> 'I am going out feet first,' said Mr Bird, a wit to the end. 'My legs have entered their eternal rest. Nurse Clock, I would have you record all this and pass it on to a daily newspaper. Nurse Clock, have you pen and paper?'
>
> The nurse, seated some distance away, reading a magazine, read the message on the printed page: *Bingo and whist drives below stairs at Balmoral.* 'I am writing out your very word,' she said.
>
> 'Then listen to this,' said William Wagner Bird, and did not

ever finish the sentence.

(p. 5)

The distinct echoes of Beckett in this passage are by no means unusual; indeed, of all Trevor's novels, *The Boarding-House* is the most strongly influenced by Beckett, particularly with Beckett's tendency to use words that seem slightly out of context, or to turn stock phrases upside down for comic or ironic effect: "The brown of the boarding-house did not, however, universally command" (p. 9); "The wet soil clattered upon the wood of Mr Bird's container" (p. 21); "She had nursed Mr Bird to his death" (p. 26). Beckett can also be seen behind some of the novel's eccentric characters: Miss Clerricot's boss, Mr Sellwood, for example, amuses himself while having drinks and dinner with Miss Clerricot by calculating with all the obsessive care of a Watt or a Molloy how long it takes the waiter to make the trip from their table to the bar and back again.

The character who indulges most freely in this kind of self-conscious discourse is Mr Bird, who, because he has created the boarding-house community, and has written extensively about it in his "Notes on Residents," is in some ways a surrogate author.[10] Mr Bird's dialogue inevitably creates ironic doubt, especially in regard to the important question of why he assembled the community in the first place. The view that he operated on essentially humanitarian impulses, for which there is considerable evidence, is qualified by several of his reported conversations, which prevent the reader from identifying with him at the same time that they raise questions about his motives. An example is this exchange with Tome Obd, reported in "Notes on Residents":

> I observed Mr Obd. His ebony face seemed strange and immensely remote in my small room. I said quietly:
> 'I am always glad to welcome an imperial cousin.'
> 'An imperial cousin?' He questioned me as though I spoke in a mysterious way, as though he did not understand our language. I said, more slowly:
> 'There is no skin prejudice in this house.'
> He, as though repetition were his forte, repeated the words.
> 'Skin prejudice?'
> 'But I must add,' I said, 'that those who come here are recommended from the highest sources. I confess it straight away, Mr Obd, we have

had foreigners here in the past. Ambassadors of foreign powers are not unknown in the precincts of the boarding-house, nor are the world's potentates, oilmen, religious leaders, mystics, men of politics, men of royal blood. The four winds have swept the great and the little, the good and the evil, into our midst here in the boarding-house –'

'Precincts?' queried Mr Obd.

'That is difficult to explain,' I said. 'Where were you at school, Mr Obd?'

Thus we went on for some time, for I delight myself by talking in this manner.

(pp. 129–30)

Although the large, crowded canvas of *The Boarding-House* tends to prohibit the kind of precise, disciplined structure that characterizes *The Old Boys* – and there are more than a few moments in this book where Trevor's fondness for eccentricity and slapstick distorts the novel's shape or impedes its narrative flow[11] – the book on the whole projects an authenticity of feeling, a truth to human experience, somewhat less evident in the earlier novel. One reason for this is that Trevor is more inclined in *The Boarding-House* to dip into a character's past to deepen characterization or heighten emotional intensity. When Miss Clerricot is having dinner with Mr Sellwood during their trip to Leeds, for example, Miss Clerricot's shattering realization that her boss is not in the least romantically interested in her is given considerable emotional force by a brief memory of a party held to honor her eighth birthday, at which she experienced extreme terror at being the center of attention. This momentary flashback provides an effective transition to carry the scene from the Beckettian comedy of Mr Sellwood's timing of the waiter to the genuine pathos and horror that accompany Miss Clerricot's sudden understanding that she has risked exposure and self-condemnation for nothing, that she will always be "what she had been: a woman whom no man had ever taken a liberty with" (p. 182).

Even some of the novel's most minor characters receive this treatment. Janice Rush appears very briefly in the book, as a potential victim of one of Mr Studdy's schemes, but a relatively extensive flashback develops her character considerably, at the same time that it reinforces the novel's concern with loss and loneliness:

Her husband, Martin Henry Rush, had married her nineteen years ago, one hot day in August in the church of St Cyril, the church of a south-western suburb. The Reverend Hamblin had conducted the service and a Mr Pryse, St Cyril's official organist, had played *Jesu, Joy of Man's Desiring* as she walked up the aisle on her father's arm. . . . It was a memory that had never ceased to comfort her: she liked to think of herself then, that day at the altar of St Cyril's and later on the lawn of the hotel, because she saw the occasion as the ultimate blooming of her innocence and the end of her girlish optimism; she saw it decorated with the lupins that had just reached their greatest beauty in the flower-beds, and her happiest memory was one in which she stood against the lupins, at her mother's request, while a bearded photographer captured the image from many angles. Later that day, when Janice and Martin Henry were in an aeroplane, the lupins began to wilt and by the following morning were well past their prime. For Janice the process was longer drawn-out; but she knew quite soon that she had lived until her wedding day and had then begun to die.

(pp. 92–3)

This is precisely the kind of characterization, minutely detailed and perfectly paced, that serves Trevor so well in his short stories; here, multiplied again and again across the surface of the novel, it creates a density of human experience unmatched in Trevor's two earlier works.

The Boarding-House also contains the most complex character in Trevor's fiction to this point – Nurse Clock. On the surface, she is a calculating, heartless woman compulsively driven to control whatever situation she finds herself in and whoever she finds herself with. Once she gets authority – through the provision in Mr Bird's will that she and Mr Studdy are to run the boarding-house after Mr Bird's death – she uses it ruthlessly, first to get rid of the boarders (in defiance of the will) so that she can convert the house into a home for the elderly, and then to get rid of Mr Studdy, her longtime enemy. "*She is a woman I would fear were it not for my superior position,*" Mr Bird says in his notes (p. 256).

And yet whatever her methods, her motives seem, at least in part, perfectly humane. In several scenes in which she is the center of consciousness, the narrative reveals a genuine selflessness behind her plans to convert the boarding-house to a rest home: "And she promised herself that in the summer months, in June and July and August, a year after Mr Bird's death, old people would take their ease in canvas garden-chairs and be happy to greet their ninetieth year" (p. 195). And later, when she is having trouble getting one of her patients, Mrs Maylam, to cooperate with her, a brief flashback reveals precisely the spirit of compassion and connection, albeit tempered by the usual overtones of irony, so central to Trevor's vision:

> There had been a day when Bishop Hode, a man in his time of education and power, had been incontinent in the airing cupboard and she had conveyed him to the bathroom. 'My love, my love,' she had cried when she saw him. 'My poor old love, you are safe with me.' And she gathered him up in her two strong arms and carried him to the bathroom and wiped away his tears of shame. She had whispered then that there was nothing to cry about, telling him the facts of life beyond the ninetieth year, and stripping him and sponging his worn old body. She would never be able to lift Mrs Maylam because Mrs Maylam weighed fourteen stone, but she could set Mrs Maylam to rights and could make it clear that the obedience she required grew out of love.
>
> (pp. 227–8)

Mr Bird's character is marked by a similar, and equally suggestive, ambiguity. At times, his notes reveal him to be a man of genuine compassion (*"Yet how can one not extend the hand of pity towards him? Anyone can see that poor old Studdy never had a friend in his life"* (p. 97)) who, in creating the boarding-house community, put into practice the principle of human connection: *"Well, at least I have done a good thing – I have brought them all together; and though they are solitary spirits, they have seen in my boarding-house that there are others who have been plucked from the same bush. This, I maintain, lends them some trifling solace"* (p. 40). Yet those qualities are offset to some extent by Mr Bird's elevated, distancing rhetoric, as was argued earlier, and by the will that he leaves behind him; the novel refuses to make clear whether the seemingly perverse choice of a Nurse Clock–Mr Studdy directorship was motivated by a belief that the task would bring these two opposites together, or by a cruel, heartless design to make sure that his own creation could not survive him:

> But no one knew that before he died, an hour or so before the
> end, Mr Bird had visualized the boarding-house as it would be
> after his time. He saw a well-run house safe in the care of his
> two chosen champions, with all its inmates intact and present,
> a monument to himself. He dozed awhile in peace, and then,
> awake, he imagined for a moment that he had died and that the
> boarding-house was dying too. He thought that someone asked
> him a question, seeking an explanation for his motives and plan-
> ning. He heard himself laughing in reply, the same soft sound,
> like water moving, and he said aloud: 'I built that I might
> destroy.'
>
> (p. 212)

The ambiguity here is thematically significant. Mr Bird's first
vision cannot be allowed to stand, any more than can the
boarding-house; both, like the faith in compassion and connection
that they suggest, must be qualified by a realistic assessment of
human nature and contemporary society. That soft laugh is, after
all, the gesture of an ironist, and Trevor certainly has proved
himself, by this point in his career, at least as worthy of the title
as is his surrogate. When the narrator says, a few pages earlier,
"Mr Bird had found that when recording the idiosyncrasies of his
residents he had been wont to do so with a ghost of a smile upon
his lips" (p. 208), the reader is surely meant to see Trevor himself
standing behind all the scenes and characters of *The Boarding-
House*, and enjoying precisely the same ironic grin.

THE LOVE DEPARTMENT

When Mr Bird used to take his daily stroll around the neighborhood of his boarding-house on Jubilee Road, he frequently walked
along Crimea Road, and so conceivably could have spotted Mr or
Mrs Jaraby coming in or going out of their house. And when
Septimus Tuam and Eve Bolsover, in *The Love Department*, cruised
through Wimbledon in Eve's small red car, they might well have
seen two more of Trevor's old boys as they rounded a corner
marked by the Rimini Hotel, home to Mr Sole and Mr Cridley.
All these early novels are set in the same southwestern, suburban
area of London, but it is only in *The Love Department* that Trevor

31

begins to investigate the one class – the middle class – that dominates and defines contemporary suburbia. More specifically, *The Love Department* is Trevor's first novel to explore middle-class marriages, and to use the breakup of those marriages as a way of dramatizing his vision of disconnection and alienation. And so it marks a development in Trevor's work that carries him away from writing about the edges of society – the very old or the very eccentric – into writing about the center of society, while providing a powerful symbol for what he sees as the principal failings of contemporary life.

Judged against some of Trevor's more mature writing on the subject – *Elizabeth Alone* and stories like "Access to the Children," "The Grass Widows," "Angels at the Ritz," and "Mrs Silly" – *The Love Department* bears some signs of apprentice-work. Trevor is still struggling for the right form and voice with which to dramatize this new area of interest, and the novel, finally, proves a somewhat unworkable mix of romance and realism. But, significantly, the most accomplished parts of *The Love Department* have to do with the middle-class marriage of James and Eve Bolsover, portrayed in a markedly more realistic vein than is anything before it in Trevor's work. One need only compare the stylized dialogues between the Jarabys with this conversation between the Bolsovers, during their tenth anniversary dinner, to see how Trevor employs a more natural language here (without abandoning entirely the nuances of Beckett and Pinter, especially their tendency to rely on what is not said) to dramatize the woes of marriage:

A waiter displayed the label on a bottle of wine, and James nodded his head. He said to his wife:
'This is a good place.'
Eve looked about her and said that the place seemed good.
'The food is good,' said James. 'Food is cooked here in a rare way. Their hazel hen, you know, is excellent. You should have had the hazel hen, my dear.'
'I have never had hazel hen. To tell the truth, I've never even heard of it.'
'It's a cheap dish and yet a delicacy. They're charging about ten times too much for it.' . . .
'My father's dying now,' murmured James.
'I know,' said his wife.

(p. 43)

Because the Bolsovers stand at the emotional center of the book, their characterization is crucial. And in Eve, Trevor has created the most intimately known, fully realized character up to this point in his work. The usual mix of perspectives provided by the novel's being structured around multiple centers of consciousness is supplemented in her characterization by frequent incursions into her consciousness and memory that build sympathy for her and, at the same time, realistically portray the feelings of frustration, futility, and waste that drive her into the eager, exploiting arms of Septimus Tuam. For example, before she takes up with Septimus, she and James host a dinner-party for some of James's fellow board-members, a farcical event that Trevor plays for all the comedy that he can squeeze out of it. But when it is over, the narrative moves inside Eve's consciousness as she thinks about the past, the other women that she has met that night, and her husband, sleeping in his chair in front of her:[12]

> One by one, the scenes passed before her: moments of her marriage day, for she continued in her obsession about it and she knew the day well. She stood about, and walked and spoke; she was there in white, saying the right thing, moving among people: the scenes were like parts of a slow film. Would she, she wondered, take to a sofa like Mrs Linderfoot, when the children had grown up and gone? Would she lie there and dream all afternoon of the distant past, of a man she had married on a sunny day? What did Mrs Linderfoot think about? Or Mrs Clinger, come to that? Or Mrs Poache?
>
> 'Oh, James,' cried Eve, running across the room and putting her arms about the form of her sleeping husband.
>
> James did not hear, nor did he move.
>
> (pp. 139–40)

In the novel's most dramatic scene, in which Septimus tells Eve that their relationship is over, it is Eve's suffering that is always in focus, even though the center of consciousness shifts from Eve to Septimus and then to an outsider:

> 'May we meet again soon?' said Eve. 'Tomorrow morning?'
>
> 'Shall we shake hands?' said Septimus Tuam, and Eve looked up at him, standing there gaunt and unsmiling, his thin face seeming more than ever like a sacred thing, his body bent at an

angle. 'Shall we shake hands?' he repeated. 'For you know, dear, it's nobody's fault in the world if all these weeks we've been at cross purposes.'

Septimus Tuam's hand was stretched out towards her, coming down from above, on a level with her head. He was thinking as he held it there that perhaps, in fairness, he should have explained that the extreme brevity of their love affair was to do with the part that Mrs FitzArthur played in his life.

People taking tea in the Bluebird Café heard weeping that afternoon such as many of them had never known could occur. A dark, narrow-jawed young man stood above a table holding out his right hand, while the woman at the table, a beautiful woman who was dark also, sobbed and moaned. She spoke some words – a plea, the people afterwards said – but the young man seemed not to be able to distinguish what the meaning was. The woman's body shook and heaved. A tea-cup was over-turned on the table-cloth.

(pp. 256–7)

That last move to a slightly enlarged perspective keeps Eve in focus and maintains the scene's emotional intensity while avoiding any tendency to lapse into sentimentality.[13]

Although James plays a smaller role in the novel than does Eve or Septimus, his suffering from the threatened breakup of his marriage is dramatized with considerable psychological realism. His frequent fantasies about losing his position on the board and being driven into poverty, for example, underscore his anxieties about his marriage at the same time that they offer a male parallel to Eve's sense of the meaninglessness of her middle-class suburban life. Also, his efforts to come to terms with the death of his father add resonance to his attempts to face the death of his marriage.

Moreover, drawing on a large and varied cast of characters, Trevor broadens the dramatization of his theme of disconnection through a series of male–female relationships that offer parallels to the Bolsover marriage. The FitzArthurs, another middle-class Wimbledon couple that fall from lethargy into the waiting hands of Septimus Tuam, enact the view that marriage is essentially a power struggle between opposed, separate wills; the one-way rela-tionship between Miss Brown and Lake, a more elaborate version of the lamentable affair between Miss Clerricot and Mr Sellwood in *The Boarding-House*, embodies the pain and pathos of unfulfilled love; Mrs Hoop's efforts to use Old Beach's affections to get his money, a lower-class version of Septimus's schemes for conning unsettled suburban housewives, suggest how compassion and love can be exploited for material gain. Also, the letters that arrive in Lady Dolores's "love department" offer sobering testimony to the suffering caused by marital disconnection: *"why do we quarrel over the clothes we wear? We quarrel about what food to give our dogs, raw meat from butchers' or food from tins. We quarrel over how to lay a table, and if powdered coffee has a drug in it. We think of separation, but now we are old: we are in our sixties now, my husband and I"* (p. 13); or *"we are polite and civilised, we do not quarrel, nor tell a joke. We simulate preoccupation, but are preoccupied only with the mistake we made in 1940. We are like funeral mutes in this house"* (p. 14). And finally there is Lady Dolores herself, a woman whose obsessive interest in the marriages of other people, and whose peculiar, deranged fascination with Septimus Tuam, suggest a severely repressed sexuality and a corruption of the principle of connection.

In dealing with much of this material, Trevor employs techniques associated with realism, and large parts of the book – especially the scenes in which the Bolsovers figure importantly – have the familiar feel of verisimilitude. But *The Love Department* also is marked by strong streaks of allegory and romance, fictional modes not much in evidence in Trevor's work before this point. Septimus, for example, can be seen as playing the allegorical role of Satan, tempting this contemporary Eve inside the seemingly safe confines of her Edenic, suburban Wimbledon. He does cast a spell over her – "Eve did not understand why she had fallen in love with Septimus Tuam as she had so clearly understood her love for James" (p. 190) – and as an apparent agent of the irrational, romantic power of love, he challenges many of the values and conventions on which the suburban middle class is founded. "He had seemed like someone who might be in a circus," Eve thinks, "and he made her feel as though she belonged there too" (p. 190).

There is, however, nothing irrational, romantic, or even imaginative about this Mephistopheles. Seen realistically, Septimus is a hard, cold, calculating con-man, bent on exploiting loneliness and the need for connection. When Trevor trains his realistic lens on Septimus, he is seen marking off the days on his calendar until, according to his careful plan, he ought next approach a particular victim, or reflecting on the £4,500 that he has accumulated in his post-office savings account, the fruits of his unscrupulous, satanic labors. In the end, however, the devil does get his due, as befits the villain in a romance; while Eve and James decide to try to patch up their marriage, Septimus is killed in an accident started, unwittingly, by the naive young man hired by Lady Dolores to track him. And since, as it turns out, no one knows his real name, Septimus Tuam passes away, like a ghost, without leaving a trace.

That naive young man, Edward Blakeston-Smith, is Septimus's allegorical opposite, a figure as angelic ("He stood before her, with his smile and his light-blue eyes, with red cheeks and fair golden hair" (p. 16)) as the dark-complexioned, dark-haired Septimus is satanic. Lady Dolores sees Edward's innocence as a potentially useful foil to Septimus ("Only innocence can match the black heart of Septimus Tuam" (p. 38)), and Eve does, as it turns out, struggle for her soul between the two of them.

As the young, innocent man who ventures out into the world of corruption, Edward also takes the part of the conventional hero of romance. The book opens with Edward at a monastery, living in retreat and innocence: "Edward knew nothing about love as he sat in the back garden of St Gregory's playing draughts with Brother Toby" (p. 7). It ends with Edward back at the monastery, withdrawn once again from the world of reality, but now burdened with a knowledge of good and evil that he cannot discard: "There would be no forgetting. He would remember for ever the facts of love as he had seen them played before him, and he would feel a sadness" (p. 295).

As always, however, Trevor's irony is working to qualify and question, and, in this instance, to remind the reader that neither idealistic notions nor idealistic modes of narrative can adequately account for the complexities and realities of contemporary life. Like all heroes of romance, Edward may seem to have moved from innocence to experience at the end of the novel, but, in the book's final irony, he is innocent of his part in the climax of the plot, the death of Septimus: " 'The cyclist rode off,' said a woman who had not spoken before. 'The cyclist was innocent' " (p. 276). Moreover, Edward's madness – and he is decidedly unhinged; he first went to St Gregory's because he could not differentiate between reality and billboard advertisements – suggests that innocence and virtue, of such angelic quality anyway, are poorly suited for survival in a world filled with creatures like Lady Dolores and Septimus Tuam.

As all this suggests, *The Love Department* is an ambitious book, both in the range of its concerns and in the variety of narrative strategies that it draws on. It also embraces a broad, heterogenous mix of comic modes, from satirical probings of middle-class social life (the dinner-party at the Bolsovers) and the world of corporate business (Lake's amoral, predatory designs on James's position; the futile activity of the board, caught up in controversies about central heating and replacing metal doorknobs in the building with china ones) to rather crude slapstick (the Clingers's pet monkey attacking Mrs Hoop at the Bolsovers's dinner-party; Lake's desperate search for a set of false teeth to replace those stamped on by Miss Brown) and to the same kind of Beckettian linguistic humor found in *The Old Boys* and *The Boarding-House* ("Failure, he felt, would surely have some pleasure after the tedium of the other" (p. 98)).

Ultimately, the book cannot quite hold all these different kinds of writing together, and Trevor has particular trouble in bridging the gap between realism and romance, psychological depth and allegorical suggestiveness; some characters, like the Bolsovers, seem to come straight out of the tradition of literary realism, while others, like Septimus and Edward, seem at times part of a morality play.[14] And yet for all its structural difficulties, *The Love Department* does carry Trevor into new fictional territory – the middle class, suburbia, love and marriage – that will, in the next few years of his career, be explored with increasing sophistication and effect.

3

"THE ODOUR OF ASHPITS":
The Middle Novels

The opening scene of *Mrs Eckdorf in O'Neill's Hotel* promises the same wryly observed comedy of eccentricity that characterizes much of Trevor's early writing: a garrulous, apparently deranged middle-aged woman, a professional photographer from Germany, has trapped a reserved Englishman on an airplane *en route* to Dublin, and is mercilessly battering him with a bewildering story about a rundown hotel in that city. The familiar trappings of Trevor's humor are, however, misleading. The story that Mrs Eckdorf tries to tell her confused travelling companion is not at all comic; it is a story about loss, exploitation, and alienation, a story full of connections gone bad. Nor is the story of Mrs Eckdorf herself – that is, the principal story of *Mrs Eckdorf in O'Neill's Hotel* – comic; the only character in the novel who argues for Forster's principle of "Only Connect," she is ignored, rejected, and, by the end of the book, driven mad.

"It would be very difficult for me to say," Trevor once remarked, "if I were to be cast away on Plumley's desert island, whether I would take Hardy or Dickens."[1] Although it over-simplifies matters somewhat to represent the difference between the world of the Jarabys or Mr Bird's boarding-house and that of Mrs Eckdorf as a shift away from Dickens and toward Hardy, Trevor's work does take a decided turn in his middle novels in the direction of the pessimistic, if not exactly the Hardyesque. In the first two of these books especially – *Mrs Eckdorf in O'Neill's Hotel* (1969) and *Miss Gomez and the Brethren* (1971) – the principle of compassion and connection affirmed in various, often comic ways in the earlier novels is all but overwhelmed by a relentlessly bleak vision in which human relationships are defined almost exclusively by exploitation, deceit, cruelty, and indifference, and in which alienated characters move about in worlds where almost everything, from landscapes to social institutions to human associations, is crumbling or in ruin. This vision, as dark in its way as the fatalism that informs *Tess of the D'Urbervilles* or *Jude the Obscure*, does not, however, completely master Trevor's imagination. Trevor's faith in compassion and connection, however threatened by the damaged, sinister worlds inhabited by Mrs Eckdorf and Miss Gomez, surfaces with new clarity and assurance in the last and most accomplished of these middle novels, *Elizabeth Alone* (1973), a book that marks the beginning of Trevor's best work as a novelist.

As their titles indicate, all three of these novels take women as their protagonists, an extension of Trevor's commitment, observed in much of his earlier work, to steer clear of autobiographical fiction. The first two novels hold to the eccentric perimeters of society that Trevor, in books like *The Old Boys* and *The Boarding-House*, staked out as his primary fictional terrain – an unstable journalist-photographer from Germany descending on a rundown Dublin hotel in search of a human-interest story, a young black woman from Jamaica trying to drum an evangelistic religious faith into the empty lives of the owners of a pub in a London neighborhood undergoing urban renewal. In *Elizabeth Alone*, Trevor explores with new depth and sensitivity the suburban middle class first taken up, in allegorical and realistic terms, in *The Love Department*, and also the subject of some of his early short stories. (Between the publication of *The Love Department* in 1966 and the appearance of *Elizabeth Alone* in 1973, Trevor published his first two volumes of short stories, *The Day We Got Drunk on Cake*, in 1967, and *The Ballroom of Romance*, in 1972.) These three novels also share an emphasis on introspection and psychological realism that is much less visible in the earlier novels. On the whole, although something is lost in the transition away from the Dickensian and Beckettian comedy of novels like *The Old Boys* and *The Boarding-House*, these three portrayals of the contemporary wasteland reveal a genuine extension and deepening of the range of Trevor's literary art.

MRS ECKDORF IN O'NEILL'S HOTEL

Although *Mrs Eckdorf in O'Neill's Hotel* is Trevor's first piece of writing set in Ireland – and although Trevor himself once described it as "a purely Irish novel"[2] – it is not principally concerned with Irish issues, as are *Fools of Fortune* and *The Silence in the Garden*, and its Dublin setting serves chiefly as a background for thematic concerns that connect the book with *Miss Gomez and the Brethren* and *Elizabeth Alone*. In that sense, *Mrs Eckdorf in O'Neill's Hotel* is indebted less to any Irish literary tradition than to a book by an Irishman that sets out to reject that tradition, Joyce's *Dubliners*. As Joyce used his own bitter perception of Dublin at the turn of the century to project a far-reaching view of modern man as paralyzed and morally corrupt, so Trevor draws on a more contemporary Dublin setting to convey his wider vision of disconnection and corruption in contemporary society as a whole.[3]

Like Mr Bird's boarding-house, O'Neill's Hotel serves as a meeting-place or connecting point for characters from different walks of life. But the comedy of missed or missing connections that helps temper the earlier book's concern with loss and alienation is replaced here by a tragedy of vital connections irreparably broken. The hotel itself, once both a gathering point for all kinds of people and a centripetal center for the Sinnott family, is now in the final stages of decay as both hotel and home. The family has been broken up and replaced by a mock-family that includes a prostitute and a pimp. Its nominal head, Mrs Sinnott, is 91 years old, deaf, and dumb – all suggesting her weakened ability to hold her family together.[4] Her son Eugene, a drunkard and a gambler, is estranged from his wife, Philomena, formerly a maid at the hotel, and from his son. The daughter of the family, Enid Gregan, is unhappily married to an insurance executive, living an Irish version of the life of the Bolsovers in a suburban area of Dublin. The hotel's porter, a lean, lonely man named O'Shea, lives pathetically on the illusion that the hotel will one day be restored to its former grandeur, despite the reality of the everyday presence of Agnes Quin, a prostitute who uses the hotel for her trade, and Morrissey, a pimp for Agnes and an accomplished, small-time con-artist.

Mrs Eckdorf's arrival in this world of disappointment, frustration, and corruption raises Trevor's concern with the conflict between the principle of compassion and connection and the reality of an alienated and alienating contemporary society. Mrs Eckdorf's journalistic mission – to tell, through a book of photographs, the story of the decline of O'Neill's Hotel and its family – is, to a limited extent, Trevor's fictional mission. But Trevor's story is primarily the story of Mrs Eckdorf, and as a journalist working on a hunch and a story she heard once from a man who had visited O'Neill's, Mrs Eckdorf is operating from ambivalent motives that themselves contain the novel's major moral conflict. On the one hand, as Mrs Eckdorf frequently asserts, her work – and she has published a number of successful books of this kind – can be seen as advancing the idea of connection and mutual responsibility by increasing social and political awareness. "We are all God's creatures," she tells the Englishman on the airplane. "We concern one another. . . . We are all part of one another, my dear, and we must know one another better."[5] On the other hand, it might be argued that Mrs Eckdorf is essentially an exploiter of human suffering, someone who makes a fat living by ruthlessly and amorally publicizing the private misfortunes of others.

For the most part, Mrs Eckdorf never gets to the bottom of the story that she comes to Dublin to find; in the end, she can only surmise the sequence of events that drove Philomena and Eugene apart and Enid out of the hotel, and that led to the demise of the business and the family. But her search for the truth of the story about O'Neill's Hotel leads her to what appears to be a discovery of truth about her own life and motives, an epiphany of sorts that is thoroughly Joycean, especially in the way in which it relies on irony to qualify or question the value of the character's self-discovery. Considering how the members of the family return to the hotel each year to celebrate Mrs Sinnott's birthday, Mrs Eckdorf becomes convinced that they are motivated principally by forgiveness and sympathy; this in turn leads to a crucial moment for her:

> She stood alone then, in the centre of her bedroom, thinking that she had come in arrogance and treachery, the woman her life had made her. Yet without knowing a thing about it, she had come so that she, too, might learn forgiveness. She would display now for all the hard world to see a human story that was

her story also: she would tell how she had felt her intuitions working and how, through the example of the people of the exercise-books and the goodness of Mrs Sinnott, she had herself been given the strength to forgive those whose victim she had been. . . . On azure-tinted photogravure paper she would show the working of a forgotten God.

(pp. 211–12)

The ironic undercutting here, accomplished partly through a Joycean overwriting, has considerable thematic importance. In all three of these middle novels, Trevor focuses on characters inspired by various kinds of evangelical zeal – Mrs Eckdorf, Miss Gomez, and, in *Elizabeth Alone*, Miss Samson – and in all of them, Trevor seems somewhat suspicious of these figures partly because of the overbearing nature of their religious beliefs, their inability to allow for the ironic, realistic qualifications so crucial to Trevor's own humanistic attitudes. In this novel, if Mrs Eckdorf is taken to be the primary agent of compassion and connection, arriving like a missionary in a world badly in need of the values that she professes, she also proves to be something of a fanatic, and she does end up in madness.

At the same time, Trevor also works to create and maintain sympathy for Mrs Eckdorf, and so for the values that she preaches. Moreover, the ambiguities of Mrs Eckdorf's character help Trevor hold his characteristic balance between affirming the need for compassion and connection and recognizing a world hostile to those values. The issue of Mrs Eckdorf's madness, for example, is clouded by the insistently posed question of who is deranged, Mrs Eckdorf or those who dismiss her as mad. "No one here can understand you," an exasperated Eugene tells Mrs Eckdorf late in the novel (p. 280), and the reader is meant to wonder who is to blame for that. Is it simply a question of a woman blinded by fanaticism to the realities of life, a woman who sees forgiveness and compassion where there is neither, or is the world to which she brings her message morally unbalanced because it has become so deaf to what she has to say? Trevor's irony constantly keeps the novel moving back and forth between these two poles. For example, one of Mrs Eckdorf's sermons about forgiveness and connection is preached to a minor character named Mr Smedley, a Liverpool businessman for whom Morrissey has provided a prostitute, and whose clothes an outraged Mrs Eckdorf has stolen:

> Mr Smedley, still with his back to her, said that he did not believe in God. He mentioned his clothes again. He said he could not stand here in this condition talking to two women about God. He had a plane to catch.
>
> 'An extraordinary thing has happened in this hotel,' said Mrs Eckdorf. 'A family has been cleansed of its crimes by a silent woman, through whom God reached out –'
>
> 'I don't care who reached out,' shouted Mr Smedley, turning suddenly and glaring at Mrs Eckdorf. 'It has nothing to do with me what happened in this hotel –'
>
> 'In that you are wrong: we are all to do with one another. We must never seek to escape one another. We are here to know one another.'
>
> 'Will you shut up that rubbish?' cried Mr Smedley. 'Are you half-witted? Are you mad? My clothes have been stolen and all you can talk about is God reaching out. I don't believe in any God.'

(p. 248)

The irony and the comedy in this scene discourage an exclusive sympathy with one side or the other; who is the most misguided here, the idealistic Mrs Eckdorf or the sordid, unfeeling Mr Smedley?

Trevor also goes to considerable lengths to portray Mrs Eckdorf as at least as much a victim of other people as an exploiter of them; her father deserted his family when she was a young girl, her first sexual experience took the form of abusive advances from a female teacher, both of her marriages have been unconsummated. Mrs Eckdorf's highly specific memories of her father, for example, clearly are designed to generate sympathy for her:

> She remembered taking her father's hand and walking with him through the streets of Maida Vale, in London. She remembered the smell of her father, an odour of tobacco, and the brownness of his hard fingers, and his mouth smiling at her. . . .
>
> In their flat in Maida Vale she gave raisins and crumbs of bread to dolls, and her father sat beside them on the floor, receiving raisins and bread as well. There was a doll that always

43

sat on her father's lap, called Janey Rose, whose hair he said he liked because she always kept it brushed. After tea-time with the dolls her father would find that he had sticks of Peggy's Leg in his pocket, or liquorice sweets. 'We'll read the dolls a story,' she would say, listening while he read aloud. And then one day her father wasn't there.

She did not see him ever after that. She asked her mother if he'd died, but her mother replied that he was still very much alive. They had agreed, she said, that none of them should meet again: she had insisted upon that, since she was being left with the burden of the child. He had decided on another wife, she explained, who did not wish to take on another woman's child.

(pp. 257–8)

Even when Mrs Eckdorf turns violent, in the scene in which, out of frustration, she strikes Morrissey on the head with a ruler, Trevor structures the narrative in such a way as to explain the action in terms of Mrs Eckdorf's psychological makeup. The blow itself is never described; instead, the narrative shifts, at the crucial moment, to Mrs Eckdorf's memory of a humiliating scene with her first husband:

Mrs Eckdorf did not hear Morrissey saying that. She was standing, while he remained seated at the desk. Beside her, on another desk, there was an ebony ruler. This she now seized.

Hoerschelmann was making the point to her that she should have told him before their marriage more about herself. He quite understood that she was a woman of talent, he said: he appreciated her art and he understood her desire to pursue the truth so that everyone, everywhere, should know more about one another. It was she herself, Hoerschelmann was saying in his loud voice: it was she herself he wished to discuss, it was she herself they should have discussed a long time before.

His voice was full of insult; his teeth were exposed in a snarling kind of way, the whole lower part of his face was sneering at her, his eyes were half-closed.

'For Jesus' sake!' cried Morrissey. His right hand was pressed to the side of his head, where the ebony ruler had struck him.

(p. 180)

Trevor's characterization of the novel's two principal low-life characters, Morrissey and Agnes Quin, is also designed to force the reader to see these characters as victims of a compassionless society, not just as victimizers. As a prostitute, Agnes Quin exploits the loneliness and frustration of others, and represents as well a perversion of the ideal of love; but she also, as Trevor makes clear by delving into her past, has been victimized and exploited herself. In the course of the longest and most detailed flashback in the novel (or in any of the novels that come before it), Trevor reveals the bizarre circumstances of Agnes's infancy – she was handed over to a convent by a man never heard from again – and then goes on to describe her first sexual experience, an encounter that might well have taken place in the pages of *Dubliners*:

At that time she used to go for walks with a boy who whispered often that he loved her, until one night, behind the Electricity Works, he had taken liberties with her unresisting body and afterwards had whispered nothing more at all. He had walked home beside her in silence and she had felt him thinking that he had performed a dirty action. After that, he wasn't on the lookout for her as he had been in the past, to suggest walks together to Poolbeg Lighthouse. She confessed the sin and accepted the penance, with the face of the boy still vivid in her mind, and his hands seeming to caress her body while the priest's voice murmured. A little while later, unable to restrain herself, she went to the shoe-shop where he worked. He was going to marry a girl from Tallagh, he said, and she wondered if he had said to himself that night behind the Electricity Works that in spite of love he could not marry her because she had not resisted, because she hadn't thought to say that what he demanded was a sin. He knelt before her in the shoe-shop, removing old shoes from her feet and placing on them new ones. The back of his waistcoat was black and shiny and there were rubber bands on his arms to protect the shirt-cuffs from the footwear of the customers. He pressed the leather of the shoes to discover where her toes were. He was happier doing that, she thought, than doing what he had done before. 'Ah God, you look great in them,' he said, and she went away with the shoes on her feet and her old ones in a paper bag.

(pp. 86–7)

The echoes between this scene and the experiences of Joyce's child-narrators or Eveline or Polly Mooney – all of whom are damaged by their pathetic illusions – are telling. Moreover, to the extent that Mrs Eckdorf's faith in compassion and connection can be seen as the greatest of all the illusions operating in a reality governed by the likes of Eugene Sinnott and Agnes Quin – and Father Hennessey, visiting Mrs Eckdorf in the mental institution near the end of the novel, does conclude that the lesson preached by Mrs Eckdorf is "too strange for any world but that of make-believe or madness" (p. 304) – *Mrs Eckdorf in O'Neill's Hotel* demands to be read, like *Dubliners*, as a bleak, despairing state-ment about the human condition.

MISS GOMEZ AND THE BRETHREN

Dublin's Thaddeus Street, the seedy, somewhat dilapidated neigh-borhood of O'Neill's Hotel, stands a long way down the social ladder from the well-kept streets and well-appointed houses of Wimbledon, the setting for *The Love Department*. In *Miss Gomez and the Brethren*, Trevor returns to London, but the urban environment that provides this novel's landscape is as far from Thaddeus Street, socially and economically, as Thaddeus Street is from Wimbledon. Crow Street, the central focus of the novel, has been reduced to a desert of rubble and ruin by an urban-renewal project; it is, as the following description of it suggests, a contem-porary wasteland in which the only meaningful activity going on is dismemberment:

> There were acres of hard, flat earth on which nothing moved, and streets that were not yet quite demolished. Rubble covered what pavements remained, paper and old cigarette packets lay thickly in the gutters, bottles rolled about. The houses that remained were shells, doors were gone, and windows; glass lay everywhere, crunched beneath the wheels of lorries. In the houses workmen shouted, and brown dust rose in clouds as walls fell thunderously down. Elsewhere, corrugated iron surrounded and separated building sites already allocated, and painted signs were rich in promises of all that was to come.[6]

In its vision of the contemporary human experience, *Miss Gomez and the Brethren* is as bleak as its setting. Almost without exception,

its characters are deluded, broken, or lifeless; its human relationships characterized by violence, perversity, racism, or indifference;
its tone flat, bleakly neutral, levelled, like Crow Street itself. If
Trevor's faith in compassion and connection is at times difficult to
locate amid the moral corruption and decay that dominate *Mrs
Eckdorf in O'Neill's Hotel*, in *Miss Gomez and the Brethren* those values
are hardly to be glimpsed at all under the rubble, human and
architectural, to be found on almost every page.[7] "Don't you
see, there's nothing at all?" Miss Gomez says at one point. "Just
awful human weakness, and cruelty passing from one person to
another? There's no pattern and no meaning, only makeshift
things. . . . We live for no reason" (p. 188).

Like O'Neill's Hotel, the Thistle Arms Pub, one of only two
buildings still standing on Crow Street, functions as a fictional
center that cannot hold. The family that runs it, the Tukes, is as
fractured and alienated as are the Sinnotts: Mr Tuke, a shell of
a man emotionally paralyzed by the realization that Prudence
Tuke is not his daughter; Mrs Tuke, a drunkard and adulterer
who fills her empty days with pathetically vicarious thrills gleaned
from pulp fiction; and Prudence, a vulnerable young woman
haunted by feelings of being rejected by her parents who drifts into
a misguided attachment to a sexually disturbed young man, Alban
Roche. The boarder at the Thistle Arms, an elderly man named
Mr Batt, is hard of hearing, and so lives in his own fog of
misunderstanding and isolation.

The design of this novel is close to that of *Mrs Eckdorf in
O'Neill's Hotel*; both books are structured around unlikely and
unfruitful confrontations between a world characterized by disintegration, alienation, and exploitation and a would-be agent of
moral reform. There are numerous similarities between Mrs
Eckdorf and Miss Gomez: both have been left lonely and bitter by
unhappy childhoods (Miss Gomez lost both her parents in a fire
when she was a young girl) and by unfortunate early sexual
experiences; both are strongly intuitive, overly imaginative
women; both are preoccupied with crimes, past or to come, of a
sexual nature; both are consumed with religious fanaticism; and
both are, to varying degrees, mentally unstable.[8] Also, as a black
woman from Jamaica living in London, Miss Gomez is at least as
alienated from the mainstream of society as is Mrs Eckdorf in
Dublin.

47

But as a bearer of a moral vision, Miss Gomez is undercut much more ruthlessly than is Mrs Eckdorf. For one thing, the religious organization that has inspired her to come to Crow Street and preach her sermons about compassion and connection is itself morally bankrupt, an agent of deceit and exploitation, as Miss Gomez discovers on her return to Jamaica at the end of the novel.[9] For another, Miss Gomez's message, whatever its inherent moral value, falls always on deaf ears. A conversation that Miss Gomez has with a black clerk in a supermarket, before she arrives at Crow Street, is characteristic of the way that Trevor dramatizes the unbridgeable gap between Miss Gomez and the world that she tries to convert, while at the same time revealing the moral failings of that world:

He'd noticed her on the street before she'd come in. She walked elegantly, he'd noticed, and was elegantly attired in a black, expensive-looking leather dress. You could do much worse, he was thinking now.

'I'm finished soon,' he said, taking a sum of money for the goods she'd purchased. 'You doing much tonight?'

Miss Gomez paused, about to leave the shop. She regarded the cashier seriously. He wanted to take her to some public house, where he would endeavour to make her drunk on rum and orangeade, a drink with which he had made other girls drunk. After that, in some secluded place, he would attempt to commit a rape on her. She saw it in his eyes as he looked at her, all of it happening in his mind. She wanted to go away, simply to shake her head and leave the supermarket, but instead she heard herself speaking, using words that were now more familiar to her than any other words she ever used.

'Will you listen to me,' she asked, 'if I tell you a little about my Church?'

The cashier still smiled. He would listen with considerable pleasure, he said, and added that she was a pretty girl. They would get on well if they went out together, he could tell her that already. Would she fancy going to a dance?

'The Brethren of the Way,' she said. 'We act through prayer and forgiveness. . . . Through forgiveness lies peace for each and every one of us. Comfort, which we need. And under-standing.'

She touched the man's hand with hers, and as their flesh met he looked at her differently: she felt him saying to himself that she was a religious maniac.

'Only through prayer,' she said. 'One for another. Do you understand?'

Casually, the man spat on the floor. He wiped his lips with the back of his hand. He nodded at her and said he hadn't been inside a church for seventeen years. He whistled a popular tune, moving away from his cash register in order to tidy a shelf. 'Ever eat this stuff?' he inquired, holding a packet of Cresta Curried Chicken with Rice.

(pp. 34–5)

Trevor's interest in writing about sexuality is evident in *The Love Department* and *Mrs Eckdorf in O'Neill's Hotel*, but as the casual, crass attitudes exhibited in this passage indicate, in *Miss Gomez and the Brethren*, sexual relations, like almost everything else, are taken to a bleak extreme; indeed, sexuality functions in this novel as a dominant, powerful symbol of contemporary society's failure to embrace compassion and connection. In the world of Miss Gomez and Crow Street, sexuality is either a psychological disturbance (Alban Roche's unhealthy interest in women's underclothes), a matter of commerce and exploitation (Miss Gomez's experiences as a strip-tease dancer and a prostitute), or a coarse, strictly physical phenomenon completely unrelated to love or affection (Mrs Tuke's acts of adultery, particularly the scene with a workman named Eddie Mercer in the men's room of the pub, an event that produced the ironically named Prudence). The novel is also permeated with reports and stories of sexual depravity, sexual licence, and sexual voraciousness.

These kinds of perversions are not simply given as symbols of the breakdown of human relationships; they also are presented and explained as symptoms of a morally diseased society. For example, Trevor's psychologically realistic portrait of Alban Roche, whose sexual deviancy provides one of the main elements of the plot (Miss Gomez sees her primary mission as preventing a sexual crime that she believes Alban is about to commit on Prudence), insists that he is at least as much a victim as a victimizer. He lost his father when he was very young (as Miss Gomez lost both her parents), and his relationship with his mother was unhealthily

49

suffocating; also, he grew up in a provincial Irish town, part of the repressive and alienating Ireland that Trevor later explores in short stories like "The Ballroom of Romance" and "Teresa's Wedding." In one of the several relatively extensive flashbacks accorded him, Alban recalls the burial of his mother, and partly in the way that it shifts between the event itself and Alban's tortured thoughts of sexuality, the scene suggests the extent to which Alban is a victim of forces over which he has little control:

> She died, and standing at her open grave he fought against his thoughts. 'Release from all bondage of sin,' murmured the voice of Father Dwyer. She'd died in pain, of a growth in her stomach: in the end she'd weighed only five stone four. Rain fell on the varnished wood of the coffin, and holy water too. He watched and heard, but in greater reality, it seemed, he stood in a room with the girl from the razor-blade factory. She showed him flowers she'd pressed between the pages of books and an album of photographs that she'd cut out of a film-star magazine; she liked Cary Grant, she said. Her fingers, red with chilblains, turned the pages of the album and by chance touched his. He put his arm round her waist, under a grey knitted jumper. She laughed. She took his hand and held it to her lips. He felt the tip of her tongue, so slight a touch it was like the petal of a daisy. Laughing again, she put his hand on her knee, where the stocking stretched most tautly. She pressed his fingers, urging him. 'Our Father,' murmured Father Dwyer, 'who art in heaven.'

(p. 86)

Miss Gomez is not only a woman, often perceived as a sex-object, but also a black woman. For Trevor, as he once said, race is one of those artificial barriers, like religion or class, that divide human beings,[10] and in this novel racial hatred is as powerful a symbol of disconnection and alienation as is the corruption of sexual relations. Trevor touches briefly on race in *The Boarding-House*, through the character of Tome Obd, but only in *Miss Gomez and the Brethren* is it a central concern. Mrs Tuke's narrow-minded, bigoted ignorance about Miss Gomez suggests one side of this ("Gomez was ridiculous and half-baked and half-witted and probably half human, but Gomez frightened her. . . all the time you felt afraid of her because she was a black savage who'd cook you and eat you as soon as she'd look at you" (p. 59)), while the conversation that Miss Gomez has with the black supermarket cashier brings out the divisive rage and anger generated on the other side ("'Man, we takes no heed of nothing,' the cashier cried, . . . 'We takes no heed of old Jew women that comes into this store and say, "How much the tapioca, Sambo?" If that black man'd take heed he'd slit the faces of them Jew-fat ladies'" (p. 36)). A world governed by such bitter, divisive hatred has little room for the God on whose behalf Miss Gomez is preaching, or for the humanistic values that she also advocates.

Racism and sexual aggression are part of an entire pattern of morally voracious behavior woven in and out of the action of this novel. One of the most terrifyingly symbolic scenes suggesting this quality is that in which an army of scavenging cats that has gathered and bred amid the ruins of Crow Street (a far more threatening group than the numerous cats lurking on the steps of Aldridge's flat in *A Standard of Behaviour*) attacks and kills Mr Tuke's pet Alsation:

> In the distance, as he entered Crow Street, the cats saw Rebel. Alone, head down, occasionally sniffing the ground, he trotted in the moonlight. Without sound, they moved from the cellar.
>
> As he passed the Crow Street Dining-Rooms they sprang at him, pinning him against a wall before he had a chance to gather himself. He snarled and tried to bite, but his defence was ineffectual. In their numbers, and new-found wildness they massacred without much effort.
>
> Quite naturally and with pleasure they tore his throat out, and then voraciously they ate. Even the kittens which had that afternoon been born ate flesh that still trailed blood. Hunched in a circle, the cats consumed their gory meal with the efficiency of the starving, clawing at bones, examining entrails. And one by one, then, they returned to their cellar.
>
> (p. 214)

A significant part of the horror in this scene can be accounted for by the gap between the violent, disturbing experience being described and the calm, detached language used to describe it. Trevor frequently employs this kind of deliberate under-writing to further the sense of moral indifference and emotional numbness that characterizes Miss Gomez's world.[11] The descriptions of her work as a strip-tease dancer and prostitute, for example, are rendered in a calculatedly levelled language; an example is this passage, detailing Miss Gomez's first sexual experience:

> In a cold room the man knelt down and put money in a gas-meter so that they could light the fire. He took his overcoat off and by way of conversation said he was in the advertising business. He showed her an advertisement in a newspaper that he took from his brief-case and said that it had been composed by the firm of which he was the managing director. A large picture showed a man and woman putting paint on a wall of a room. It was, the man said, an advertisement for a brand of tea.
>
> When the room warmed up they took their clothes off and lay together in the bed. They smoked cigarettes after the man had satisfied himself. . . .
>
> At half-past three he put on his clothes again, saying he'd have to be getting on. He'd already paid her the agreed price, but as a parting gift he gave her the Canadian Pacific bag which contained, he said, some cheese.
>
> (pp. 21–2)

Miss Gomez and the Brethren has a relatively small cast of characters, and relies on fewer centers of consciousness than do most Trevor novels, especially *Mrs Eckdorf in O'Neill's Hotel* and *Elizabeth Alone*. Trevor does, however, at times use multiple perspectives specifically to advance the novel's bleak conception of the unbridgeable gap between the principle of compassion and connection and the reality of contemporary life. Miss Gomez's most important moment is the long, impassioned speech that she delivers to the Tukes in the hall of the Thistle Arms, with Mr Batt and Atlas Flynn, an Irish laborer working in Crow Street who has been trying to seduce Mrs Tuke, looking on; Miss Gomez warns the Tukes that their daughter is in danger because of Alban Roche, and, more generally, makes her argument for increased understanding and forgiveness in the world. Whatever the inherent value of this argument, Trevor structures the scene to emphasize the extent to which it cannot be communicated; Miss Gomez's remarks are constantly juxtaposed with the perspectives of her listeners, who are morally if not, like Mr Batt, literally deaf. The following, typical passage from the scene, in which Miss Gomez tries to explain Alban Roche's unhealthy preoccupation with his mother, depends on a dark comedy of confusion to suggest the impossibility of Miss Gomez's being understood:

> 'At the end of my journey,' Miss Gomez said, 'was Alban Roche and your daughter. Alban Roche, whose mother's teeth are in that room upstairs.'
>
> 'Teeth?' said Mrs Tuke, considerably startled, unable to prevent herself from raising her eyes.
>
> 'The mother's teeth, wrapped up in tissue paper. The sponge the mother cleaned herself with. Her hairpins and a comb, and a brush with hair on it, and a bag of insoles. Perspiration rolled down her legs and ended up in those insoles. Every day she put those hairpins in her hair. That woman's dead and yet that woman concerns us more than ever.'
>
> Atlas Flynn gave a loud laugh, thinking it was the best thing he could do, since they could be stuck here for an hour listening to a black who was round the screw. She was a good bit of gas certainly, but he was anxious to make a definite arrangement with Beryl Tuke before he left the premises. No one seemed capable of controlling the black, who was saying the first thing that came into her head, about brothels and stripping clubs and clergymen, and was now opening up a new subject, to do with a dead woman's perspiration. The elderly party was oblivious to everything apparently, with his pipe and his Jackpot. The bearded Tuke was as grim as a priest on the stairs, looking as though he maybe fancied the black, and Beryl herself had a wonky appearance about her, like a woman he'd seen once who'd been run into by a lorry.
>
> (pp. 129–30)

The shift to Flynn's point of view in that last paragraph not only jolts the narrative into the rough, crude language of Flynn's world, but also forces a reviewing of the entire scene in terms that reveal how little chance Miss Gomez, or her moral point of view, has in such a world.

"What good was a pattern and a meaning if no one wanted to know?" Miss Gomez asks not long after this scene. "What good was a God that no one could be bothered with?" (p. 186). These questions could be said to define the vision of *Miss Gomez and the Brethren*, certainly the bleakest of Trevor's novels. And although he will, in his next novel, *Elizabeth Alone*, begin climbing out of this slough of despondency, he will never leave it completely behind him.

ELIZABETH ALONE

Trevor's best writing as a novelist begins with *Elizabeth Alone*. Not only does this book present a broader, more varied canvas than do any of Trevor's novels that come before it – ranging with facility between the suburbs of the upper-middle classes to down-and-out city streets worked by con-artists and petty criminals – but also it achieves considerably more depth than any preceding book in Trevor's canon: more psychological authenticity than anything found in *The Love Department* or in the earlier, largely comic novels, and a more fully rounded and sympathetic conception of human nature than that which governs *Mrs Eckdorf in O'Neill's Hotel* and *Miss Gomez and the Brethren*.

The lives of the novel's central characters, four very different women brought together for a short time in a ward of a London women's hospital, represent many of the concerns of Trevor's fiction – broken marriages, incomplete families, failed lovers, the elderly, religious fanaticism, petty crime and exploitation, sexual repression or deviancy – and reach into almost every class or style of life in contemporary England. They also dramatize, each in its own way, the experience of alienation and loneliness.

Elizabeth Aidallbery's recent divorce, prompted in part by an ultimately fruitless love-affair with a married man, has made her realize that her entire marriage was a waste, and her upper-middle-class suburban life a tissue of disconnected experiences, "something that was scattered untidily about," as she thinks, "without a pattern, without rhyme or reason."[12] At the age of 41, she is facing, for the first time in her life, the prospect of being alone – without husband, lover, or, in the not too distant future, her three children. Elizabeth's feelings of alienation and loss are extended through one of the principal figures in her life (and in the novel), her childhood friend Henry, a man whose life has been running downhill ever since his schooldays. Henry too has been recently divorced, and feels estranged from his 5-year-old son. He also is still hopelessly in love with Elizabeth, who turns down a proposal of marriage from him. Moreover, all his naively optimistic plans for a new start in business, for moving beyond his demeaning job as a vending-machine operator, are doomed from the beginning.

Like Miss Gomez and a number of other Trevor characters, Lily Drucker is an orphan. More important, her marriage to a shy, young librarian named Kenneth has been all but suffocated by Kenneth's parents, especially his mother, an incorrigible, garrulous woman bent on dominating her husband, clinging to her son, and destroying her daughter-in-law. The marriage of Kenneth's parents functions in the novel as a lower-middle-class version of the broken, alienating marriage of Elizabeth and her husband; the Druckers are married in name only, and their relationship has disintegrated into a barely discernible connection between a resigned husband glued to the television set and a crude, mean-spirited, brow-beating wife. Another sign of the trouble between Kenneth and Lily is that Lily has had several miscarriages.

Although she is just 25, Sylvie Clapper is, like Elizabeth, in the hospital for a hysterectomy; and whereas Elizabeth's operation suggests the loss of her past life as a wife and lover, Sylvie's insures the loss of her future in the same terms. Alienated from her unloving working-class family ("Her parents didn't mind when Sylvie went. At first she used to go back and see them, but often they weren't in when they'd said they'd be, so in the end she just stopped going" (p. 72)), she has jumped from this emotional vacuum all too eagerly into the deceitful, calculating arms of a young Irishman named Declan. A con-artist in the tradition of Studdy and Morrissey, Declan is both victimizer and victim; his callous abandonment of Sylvie is turned back against him through the even more manipulating machinations of Maloney, a fellow-Irishman and loan shark.

The life of Miss Samson, an elderly woman who has devoted herself to religion with the same zeal that inspires Mrs Eckdorf and Miss Gomez, dramatizes alienation through religious doubt. As Elizabeth has been made to feel disconnected and vulnerable because of her divorce, and Lily because of the undermining pressure exerted by Kenneth's mother, and Sylvie because of Declan's disappearance, so Miss Samson suddenly finds herself alone and uncertain spiritually when she discovers an entry in the diary of the late Mr Ibbs, her former landlord and source of religious inspiration, revealing that he had lost his faith.

Although she does not receive significantly more attention than do the three women sharing the hospital ward with her, Elizabeth is the central figure in the novel, principally because it is chiefly through her character and the changes that it undergoes that Trevor dramatizes his qualified, humanistic faith in the principle of connection and compassion. And Elizabeth's character is more convincingly realized than is that of Mrs Eckdorf or that of Miss Gomez. This probably owes more than a little to Trevor's growing achievement in the short story; between the publication in 1966 of *The Love Department*, his previous novelistic treatment of middle-class marriages, and that of *Elizabeth Alone* in 1973, Trevor published a number of highly accomplished short stories on the subject ("Access to the Children," "The Grass Widows" and "O Fat White Woman," for instance, all first appearing in *The Ballroom of Romance*, 1972). To a significant extent, it is the short-story writer's ability to dramatize a wide range of emotions in a relatively small space that accounts for the emotional impact and psychological authenticity of many of the scenes in *Elizabeth Alone* – for instance, this one, in which Elizabeth recalls the day she told her husband that she wanted a divorce:

'You're dessicated,' she'd shouted at him, weeping when she said she wanted a divorce. He was fifty-one then, tall and upright, still with his eagle's face, not taking her out to tea anymore. He stood quite still when she told him that she wanted a divorce, then he turned his back and looked through the french windows into the garden. 'I just want a divorce,' she said, knowing as she said it that it was more than that. It was more than loving someone else and wanting to have another marriage: she resented with a bitter passion the years she'd wasted with a man who'd married her because she was beautiful and young, so that she might listen and he could feel proud. The years were like useless leaves, dead now, yielding no memories that she wanted. There should be more than three children to show for nineteen years of a marriage, she cried with violence in her voice. And when he interrupted her, icily pointing out that she was endeavouring to justify her dirty weekends with grand but meaningless talk, she shouted at him again that he was dessicated. 'Maybe,' he said. 'Yet you haven't done badly out of me.'

(p. 13)

The expert modulation here between the concretely remembered moment and Elizabeth's feelings and thoughts about it enables the passage to cover a considerable amount of emotional background, all of it thematically important, in a relatively short space.

Like Mr Bird's boarding-house, O'Neill's Hotel, and the Thistle Arms Pub, the Cheltenham Street Women's Hospital functions in this novel as a connecting-point, a meeting place for characters from different classes and ways of life. For Elizabeth, her encounters in the ward with Lily, Sylvie, and Miss Samson – none of whom she might be expected to engage seriously in the course of her ordinary, relatively class-isolated life – tend to force her out of her feelings of alienation and aloneness. At first, the links between the four women in the ward are largely superficial, tending to be outweighed by the considerable personal and social differences between them. But the bonds are tested and then strengthened as each of the women experiences a devastating loss or disturbance in their lives: Henry's sudden death and the decision of Elizabeth's oldest daughter, Joanna, to leave home and live in a commune with her boyfriend; Kenneth's break with his parents and his confession to Lily about his slightly soiled earlier sexual life; Declan's unexpected, unexplained abandonment of Sylvie; Miss Samson's tortured attempts to come to terms with the implications of Mr Ibb's loss of faith, and with her own, only recently realized, romantic feelings for Mr Ibbs.

Henry's death is the first catalyst, forcing the women either to turn to each other or, at the very least, to see their own lives in the somewhat consoling perspective of the lives of others:

> Elizabeth continued to be upset, and so in a different way did Miss Samson.
>
> 'I can't pray,' Miss Samson whispered, touching Elizabeth's hand. 'I can't pray any more. That poor man.' And then Miss Samson told Elizabeth about finding the diary. She told her because Elizabeth was an outsider, unconnected with Number Nine. She asked her not to tell anyone else. She repeated to Elizabeth the words Mr Ibbs had written and said they'd caused her to have a terrible nightmare. 'I'm so sorry,' she said, touching Elizabeth's hand again. 'I'm so sorry, Mrs Aidallbery.'
>
> Lily wrote to Mrs Drucker, saying she'd rather not be visited

for a while at least, but her difficulties with her mother-in-law seemed slight compared with what had happened elsewhere. And to Sylvie the continued absence of Declan was slight in comparison also.

(pp. 266–7)

Only after she has been released from the hospital does Elizabeth begin to understand fully the significance of what has happened there. At first, in the weeks immediately following her operation, she retreats into a neutral, deliberately dissociated life, going through the motions, taking care of her house and children. "I'm trying to live quietly," she tells Miss Samson the day she visits her at the boarding-house on Balaclava Avenue where she lives. "I don't really want to talk like this. I just want to look after the children, to put things in the washing-machine and take them out again, to weed the garden" (p. 322). Miss Samson is the primary agent of moral change in the novel, the character who, despite her own personal eccentricities, eventually brings Elizabeth out of this solipsistic indifference and into an understanding of the need for compassion and connection.[13] There are significant differences between Miss Samson's advocacy of these values and that of her predecessors, Mrs Eckdorf and Miss Gomez. First, although her life has been devoted to her faith, she could not be described as a religious fanatic; in fact, at the time that she has the crucial interview with Elizabeth near the end of the novel she has lost her faith in the religious doctrines once preached by the late Mr Ibbs, and so the values that she argues for define an essentially humanistic faith offered in response to religious doubt. Second, Miss Samson has a more or less sympathetic audience. Unlike Mrs Eckdorf, who ends up babbling in a mental institution to an ineffective priest, and Miss Gomez, who is portrayed from the beginning to the end as an ineffective victim of illusions, Miss Samson speaks with the authority of having come through a dis-illusioning experience, and she has a decided effect on the novel's principal character: "In the warm sitting-room [of Miss Samson's boarding-house] the compassion of Miss Samson affected her, and seemed extraordinary. She felt ashamed that she'd so rudely tried to leave after only ten minutes, and that she'd then become irritated and had spoken so unpleasantly. The compassion of Miss Samson bewildered Elizabeth. It felt precious in the warm sitting-room, yet it also seemed unnatural, as if it were part of a miracle itself'' (pp. 328–9). Although this moment, if it can be called an epiphany at all, is a qualified one (Elizabeth is more "bewildered" than converted, and still sees Miss Samson's views as "unnatural"), and although she later thinks that "the unnatural compassion of a woman she'd met in a hospital had in no way changed the circumstances of her existence" (p. 332), her encounter with Miss Samson and her experience in the hospital in general have changed the way that Elizabeth looks at her life: among other things they have pushed her beyond her earlier, solipsistic feelings of alienation, supplying a broader perspective that in turn leads to a new strength and self-confidence. The closing lines of the novel define this position:

> It was nice to think of everything going on. . . . One day Joanna might marry someone and live in this house, and perhaps the house still wouldn't change much. One day they'd all pack her off to a Sunset Home, and Lloyd's and Midland would still race on the Thames, and London would not be much different. The Cheltenham Street Women's Hospital would be there for a bit longer, and Nine Balaclava Avenue, and the room in Shepherd's Bush that Sylvie had illicitly shared with Declan, and the small terraced house where the Druckers' sewing-machines rattled, and Meridian Close. Other drama would develop in all those places. Other women would make do, with the dazzle gone out of their marriages, or on their own because they'd never been dazzled in the first place, or had never been asked, or because things had fallen apart. Other daughters would go away, and return to apologise and forgive, and no doubt go away again. In the King of England other men would drink their way into oblivion. Other lovers would love in the Casa Peppino. Other people would be burnt in the Putney Vale Crematorium.
>
> 'One of these days,' Joanna said, 'you should marry again yourself. You sometimes look sad, you know.'
>
> Elizabeth laughed. She knelt to pick some dock from a rose-bed. She was happy enough alone, she said.
>
> (pp. 335–6)

Elizabeth alone at this point is not the same as the Elizabeth alone encountered at the beginning of the novel. And if the affirmation of connection and compassion dramatized through the changes in her character seems qualified and somewhat unspectacular, it might be argued that it is, given the world as portrayed by Trevor, all the more credible for that reason.[14]

It is not surprising that *Elizabeth Alone* ends inside its heroine's mind; the book begins there as well, with a 7-page-long, entirely introspective portrait of Elizabeth, following her thoughts and memories as her mind impressionistically traces its way through the past, and establishing with considerable conviction the psychological ground of her alienation. In fact, this novel as a whole is written out of a far more sustained and serious commitment to psychological realism than is anything in Trevor's canon that precedes it. The characterization of Henry, for example – arguably the most fully realized male character in Trevor's work[15] – is a product in large part of an unusually heavy reliance on interior modes of writing. Much more passive and benevolent than other Trevor victims – Francis Tyte, Basil Jaraby, or Alban Roche, for instance – Henry is none the less a loser, and his attempts to remake his life, inspired by an indefatigable romanticism, are undermined ultimately by the indifference of the compassionless, isolating society in which he moves, from the neighbors who dismiss him as a middle-class bum to the business associates who express no interest in him personally to his school-day friends Darcy and Carstairs, both doctors now, who pass the time with him in a pub, but exclude him from their world of professional and social success. Henry's death is, fittingly, an accident in which he is a passive victim; the day after he disasterously crashes Carstair's bridge party, drunk and dazed, he turns on the gas to heat his oven for dinner, forgets to light it, passes out on the floor, and never recovers. The entire scene, one of the most moving and convincing in all of Trevor's work, depends considerably for its effect on its introspective and retrospective revelations of Henry's character. The scene is also remarkable for its shift near the end from a third-person, but closely sympathetic narrator to direct interior monologue:

> From as far back as he could remember, right up until the day he'd made ninety-three not out in the second innings, everything had been happy. There'd been happiness with his parents, listening to his father's jokes, sleeping in the garden in

a tent he and his father had put up, telling his mother all the things he one day intended to do. Even at Miss Henderson's and Miss Gamble's Kindergarten there'd been happiness, because Miss Henderson and Miss Gamble had liked him. He hadn't worked hard enough for them, sometimes he hadn't worked at all, but even so they'd liked him. *A happy disposition* someone had written on a report at Anstey Grange.

You couldn't go back to that. You didn't have to at the moment because you were sitting in a kitchen with most of a bottle of Haig whisky inside you, almost as drunk as you could possibly be. You were forty-one years of age and ever since that last walk back to the pavilion you'd made a bog of every single thing. You'd made a bog of it because it wasn't worth making anything else of it. It was dreary and grey and full to the brim of Mrs Passes wanting two pounds for a lawnmower, and a tired woman waving from the window of mock-Tudor flats, and Felicity thinking it amusing when a man of forty-one wanted to sit in his kitchen with her. . . . All the way to the pavilion there'd been clapping, but when you were drunk in your kitchen you had to tell the truth: you couldn't cope with it because you didn't like it. There'd been clapping, and that had been that.

(pp. 257–8)

Although *Elizabeth Alone* frequently employs this kind of verticality, it is also a novel of unusual scope and breadth. Moreover, despite the large, Dickensian canvas, and a plot that moves in and out of the lives of an astonishing variety of characters, the book rarely seems sketchy or thin in its characterization. In part this stems from Trevor's tendency, observed in earlier novels, to construct his characters and scenes, however minor, out of highly specific details, giving the book as a whole a feeling of weight and density. For example, Mr Alstrop-Smith, the doctor who operates on Elizabeth, is characterized comically by a habit of recalling, while at the operating table, train journeys that he has taken. What makes the description characteristically Trevor's is the amount of specific detail lavished on it:

He cut again, the scalpel sliding through tissue with assured control. His eyes were steady. Behind the mask, his lips were tightly clamped together. His mind traversed familiar ground.

You left Victoria at nine thirty in the morning, you were in Paris Nord at five twenty-five. You left Paris Lyon at six twenty-two, you were in Rome at nine fifty-five the following morning: the Palatino, via Modane and Turin, a beautiful train. You left Victoria at three thirty, you were in Sezana at nine nineteen the following night, and in Skopje at four seventeen the next afternoon, and in Istanbul at ten past nine the morning after that. In the large, empty bar of the Pera Pallas you could sit for ever, a stranger among the Turks, drinking White Horse whisky. In Cairo your clothes stuck to you, in Athens it could be windy in October. In Segesta, if it was cold, the station-master would turn on an electric fire, a stout, kind station-master, not at all obliged to heat up a waiting traveller. It was a family concern, the railway-station at Segesta: the station-master's grandchildren ran about, his son wrote out the ticket if you left your luggage, his daughter grew flowers. . . .

He stitched. He hated stitching. One day it would be a thing of the past. Funny, in twenty years not to have come to terms with stitching flesh. He nodded, and received a scissors.

(pp. 114–15)

The comedy that lies not very far below the surface of this passage is not all that unusual in this book. In fact, one has to go back to *The Boarding-House* or *The Old Boys* to find a Trevor novel that, for all its serious moral concerns, is so frequently funny. This strong comic dimension tends also to humanize or soften the book's visions – especially in comparison with the two relatively grim novels that precede it. The following scene, for example, in which Mrs Orvitski, the woman looking after Elizabeth's children while she is in the hospital, remembers a night in which Henry's car had a flat tyre while he was driving her home, is marked by the same kind of unbridled circumstantial and linguistic comedy that distinguishes Trevor's earliest, and most humorous, novels:

'I'll have to jack you up, old girl,' he'd said the night he'd given her a lift and she'd thought at first, having never heard the expression before, that he was going to put his hands on her. She'd gripped her handbag, preparing herself to strike him on the side of the head as soon as he started anything. She'd tried to open the door of the car but there was something the matter with the catch, and before she could make any sense of it he'd got out of the car himself. A moment later she'd felt herself being raised in the air and he was shouting at her that it wouldn't take a jiffy.

(p. 37)

To say that the comic spirit is alive and well in *Elizabeth Alone* is to go a long way toward defining its essential difference from *Mrs Eckdorf in O'Neill's Hotel* and *Miss Gomez and the Brethren*. It is also to say that, although all three of these middle novels take Trevor into considerably darker corridors of human experience than any explored in his earlier books, the proper touchstone for *Elizabeth Alone* is less the dour, bitter Joyce of *Dubliners* – the man who described the Dublin of his times as permeated with "the odour of ashpits and old weeds and offal"[16] – than the more compassionate, more humane, and more humorous Joyce of *Ulysses*. And at bottom the faith in compassion and connection that counters Trevor's sightings of ashpits and old weeds and offal in the contemporary moral landscape is all but interchangeable with Joyce's faith in what Leopold Bloom, during that most trying conversation in Barney Kiernan's pub, describes in his own direct, eloquently simple way:

  – But it's no use, says he. Force, hatred, history, all that. That's not life for men and women, insult and hatred. And everybody knows that it's the very opposite of that that is really life.
    – What? says Alf.
    – Love, says Bloom. I mean the opposite of hatred.[17]

4

"OTHER PEOPLE'S PAIN":
The Late Novels

If, as Trevor once said, there are two kinds of novelists, "those who write out of curiosity, curiosity about situations and people, and those who tend to be much more autobiographical,"[1] there can be little doubt which category Trevor belongs to. One of the most striking characteristics of Trevor's fiction – witness the elderly characters in *The Old Boys* and *The Boarding-House* and the female protagonists of all three middle novels – is his capacity for writing outside his own experience. In *The Children of Dynmouth* (1976) and *Other People's Worlds* (1980), Trevor's curiosity leads him to new situations and people – a 15-year-old boy from the wrong side of the tracks in a provincial seaside town, a middle-aged widow living a life of genteel retirement in a tranquil village in Gloucestershire, and a deranged, alcoholic woman adrift amid the debris of contemporary London's seedy underside. Moreover, these two novels – from their depth of characterization to the efficacy of their narrative structures, from their commitment to social realism to their ability to dramatize and convey a coherent moral vision of contemporary man – represent the culmination of Trevor's work in the English novel.

More efficiently constructed than is the novel to which they are closest thematically, *Elizabeth Alone*, these novels take to their most accomplished limits the narrative strategies that have become hallmarks of Trevor's fiction, especially the use of juxtaposition and confrontation. They also are thoroughly and effectively shaped by Trevor's humanistic values. The plot of *The Children of Dynmouth* turns on invasions by its adolescent protagonist, Timothy Gedge, of the lives of other people, ending in an awareness both of the extent to which that community is governed by illusion and alienation and of the counterpointing need for human responsibility and compassion. The overall narrative design of *Other People's Worlds* rests on juxtapositions of radically different characters and values, and the novel is shot through with complex patterns of parallels, echoes, and foreshadowings, all working to assert the importance of connection. More specifically, the plot of *Other People's Worlds* hinges chiefly on the movement of an upper-middle-class character (Julia Ferndale) out of her world of social privilege and moral complacency and into unsettling encounters with a lower-class world defined by alienation and exploitation (Francis Tyte) and by disillusionment and despair (Doris Smith).

These two novels also exhibit a stronger social consciousness than do any of Trevor's earlier books. *Elizabeth Alone*, with its wide social spectrum, is certainly aware of social issues, but in *The Children of Dynmouth* and *Other People's Worlds*, Trevor's broad vision of contemporary man as alienated and disconnected is pointedly cast in terms of criticism of the class system. Trevor goes to considerable lengths to portray Timothy Gedge as a victim of that system, someone who is already, at the age of fifteen, locked in a fixed grid that points with deadening certainty to a lifetime of working-class drudgery. Timothy's confrontations with people in classes above his own represent both his attempt to advance his own pathetically naive ambitions to break out of his class by becoming a television comedian, and at the same time his need, conscious or otherwise, to exact some kind of revenge on the system that has crippled him. In *Other People's Worlds*, Julia's ill-advised marriage to Francis, whose origins are working-class, plunges her into a confrontation defined in large part by class differences as wide as the distance between the tranquillity of Julia's Gloucestershire and the chaos of Doris's London.

In both these novels, the "criminal" characters, Timothy and Francis – part of a long line of such figures in Trevor's fiction, going as far back as Basil Jaraby in *The Old Boys* and as far forward as Mr Maloney in *Elizabeth Alone* – are anything but minor figures; they are thematically crucial centers of focus, and their frequent presence and narrative importance keep in the foreground of each novel the disaffection and disconnection that they embody. Also, both these novels contain scenes as disturbing as anything to be found on the most desolate stretches of Thaddeus Street or Crow Street: Timothy coming upon his mother in bed with the local pub owner, for instance, or Francis taking a homosexual that he has picked up while cruising the Piccadilly Circus area to a nearby garage or a parked car.

None the less, both books assert, more forcefully than does any of Trevor's earlier fiction, a final faith in the spirit of connection and human responsibility. For better or worse, Timothy Gedge represents the future, as does Francis's and Doris's 12-year-old daughter named, ironically, Joy, and Trevor ends each novel with a commitment on the part of an adult in a higher class to the welfare of these not-so-innocent social waifs. That Trevor embodies his humanistic hopes for the future in the damaged lives of these two children – in Lavinia Featherston's plans to rehabilitate Timothy, and Julia's decision to try to rescue Joy from the hopeless future facing her – testifies both to his faith in compassion in a contemporary world defined by alienation, and to his ironic recognition that any such faith faces long odds in such a world.

THE CHILDREN OF DYNMOUTH

Trevor's eighth novel opens with a panoramic description of an apparently tranquil seaside village on the Dorset coast. With its teashops, promenade, and pier, Dynmouth attracts a modest number of tourists, lured by the sea and the promise of a relatively unspoiled environment. For many of its slightly more than 4,000 residents, the prospects are somewhat less attractive; a sandpaper factory, a tile-works, and a fish-packing station employ a fair number of them, and there are plans for a new factory that will produce lampshades. Housing ranges from a few solitary, splendid big houses to the banal council estates and dismal riverside cottages of the less fortunate. There are three banks, five places of worship, nine hotels, nineteen pubs, and, next door to the steam laundry, a fish-and-chips place known as Phyl's Phries.

This quite ordinary provincial village seems, on the surface, considerably less morally bankrupt than its nearest fictional neighbor, the tawdry, violent Brighton of Graham Greene's *Brighton Rock*, and Trevor's young protagonist, Timothy Gedge, seems less thoroughly corrupted than Greene's incorrigible Pinkie. But the ordinariness of Dynmouth, so strongly suggested in the book's opening, masks a community that is crippled by the class system and governed by alienation and deceit. Timothy, the product of a broken family, a failed school system, and a culture defined primarily by daytime television, is both a symbol of those qualities and the agent of their unmasking. Dressed in clothes that set him apart – yellow jeans, yellow tee-shirt, yellow jacket – Timothy is endowed with an uncanny ability to see through illusion and pretence, to see that, in many ways, the true children of Dynmouth are its adults, living in a moral world carefully designed to hide the truth: Mrs Abigail, with her unquestioning loyalty to her husband, a screen that prevents her from looking too deeply into why her marriage of thirty-six years has never been consummated; Commander Abigail, whose brisk cheerfulness and manly demeanor covers up the homosexual tendencies that explain his failed marriage; the quiet, self-effacing Mr Dass, a retired banker trying to keep at bay the knowledge that his family has been shattered by his son's recent departure and disavowal of his parents; Mr Plant, the owner of a local pub, whose private life is consumed with sexual infidelity; Quentin Featherston, the local rector, shaken by serious doubts as to the validity of his work and his religious beliefs; and his wife, Lavinia, on the surface the model rector's wife, but underneath a woman on the verge of psychological collapse because she can have no more children. All these characters are Timothy's "victims," and all are forced, through their dealings with him, to face, if only for a moment, the underlying truths of their lives and their community.

Timothy's overt motive for harassing these citizens of Dynmouth is that he needs certain materials from them for a one-man comedy routine that he wants to put on at the local "Spot-the-Talent" show, an event that he hopes will propel him out of Dynmouth and into television stardom. If that ambition reveals the child's side of Timothy's character, the subject of his planned show – "Brides of the Bath," three women killed by a murderer named George Joseph Smith – suggests the less innocent, more sinister side. (In *Other People's Worlds*, Trevor will develop another story of murder, the Constance Kent case, into a full symbolic subplot.) Timothy's lack of moral values is demonstrated by his willingness to use whatever means seem necessary to his end: to force the Abigails to loan him a suit of clothes, he threatens to make public the truth about the Commander's homosexuality; he confronts the Dasses with the truth about their son – information

gleaned by listening at a window of the Dass house one night –
in an effort to badger Mr Dass into getting stage-curtains for him;
he more or less tries to blackmail Mr Plant into helping him get
a tub that he needs by threatening to tell Mrs Plant about her
husband's extramarital sex life; and he terrorizes Stephen and
Kate Fleming, two 12 year-olds from well-to-do families, into
giving him Stephen's mother's wedding dress.

Timothy's covert motives are more complex, and more significant in terms of the novel's vision of contemporary society. It is
no accident that Timothy's victims are higher up on the social
ladder than he is, nor that in his dealings with Stephen and Kate,
whose privileged upper-middle-class lives are everything that
Timothy's life is not, he is at his most malicious. Timothy's treatment of the Abigails causes them much distress; but what he tells
them about the Commander's sexual preferences is, after all, true,
and he discloses it only after the Commander gets him drunk. But
the story that he plants in Stephen's and Kate's innocent minds
– that Stephen's father murdered his wife so that he could marry
Kate's mother, with whom he had been carrying on an adulterous
relationship – is not true. Moreover, in talking to Stephen and
Kate, Timothy deliberately tries to shock them out of the cocoon
of their privilege, and to undermine the relationship between
them, things that Timothy can only envy:

'Your mum on a honeymoon?' he said.
She nodded. In France, she said. Smiling, he turned to
Stephen.
'Your dad'll enjoy that, Stephen. Your dad'll be all jacked
up.'
'Jacked up?'
'Steaming for it, Stephen.'
He laughed. Stephen didn't reply.
His face was like an axe-edge, Kate thought, with another
axe-edge cutting across it: the line of the cheekbones above the
empty cheeks. His fingers were rather long, slender like a girl's.
'Your mum has a touch of style, Kate. I heard that remarked
in a vegetable shop. I'd call her an eyeful, Kate. Peachy.'
'Yes.' She muttered, her face becoming red because she felt
embarrassed.
'He knows his onions, Stephen? He's a fine man, your dad,

they're well matched. "It's great it happened," the woman in the shop said, buying leeks at the time. "It's great for the children," she said. D'you reckon it's great, Kate? D'you like having Stephen?"[2]

As Mrs Blakey, the housekeeper at the Fleming residence, thinks when she sees Timothy and the children together, Timothy, although a familiar enough sight on the street, "looked like something from another world in the garden" (p. 140), and no one is more conscious of this than Timothy himself.

The class system that generates such divisions can be seen as a manifestation of the broader principle of disconnection, and Timothy's life embodies both the evils of the social system and that larger principle. At the end of the novel, after he has abandoned his illusions about becoming a professional comedian, Timothy recognizes the truth about himself, as he has caused so many others to do about themselves – that his life is shaped by social forces beyond his control. "They're no use to me, Mr Feather," he tells Quentin Featherston when asked to leave Kate and Stephen alone. "Opportunity won't knock, sir. I'll get work in the sandpaper factory. I'll maybe go on the security" (p. 202). Quentin's projection of what lies ahead confirms this view of Timothy as a victim of the class system:

> The boy would stand in court-rooms with his smile. He would sit in the drab offices of social workers. He would be incarcerated in the cells of different gaols. By looking at him now you could sense that future, and his eyes reminded you that he had not asked to be born.
>
> (p. 207)

But the fact of Timothy's existence, of the distorted and seemingly determined nature of his life, disturbs Quentin in more profound ways: "the story of Timothy Gedge seemed to be there to mock him," he thinks. "The story wasn't fair. You couldn't understand it and mockingly it seemed that you weren't meant to: it was all just there, a small-scale catastrophe" (p. 210). Timothy is a destroyer of illusion, and therefore a seer of truth. And the truth that he brings to light is not very encouraging, at least to someone wanting to believe in man's capacity for Christian charity. For example, although the story that Timothy tells

Stephen and Kate is not literally true – Stephen's father did not push his wife over the cliff – it comes uncannily and disturbingly close to the reality, one that hardly gives grounds for an optimistic assessment of human nature: Stephen's father and Kate's mother were lovers, Stephen's mother knew about it, and her death was quite possibly a suicide. It is this kind of instinctual perception of the underside of human nature that unsettles Quentin:

> The children who had suffered a trauma would survive the experience, scarred by it and a little flawed by it. They would never forget that for a week they had imagined the act of murder had been committed. They would never see their parents in quite the same way again, and ironically it was apt that they should not, because Timothy Gedge had not told lies entirely. The grey shadows drifted, one into another. The truth was insidious, never blatant, never just facts.
>
> (p. 207)

If, as Mrs Abigail says, Timothy is a truth-teller ("Only the truth had passed from Timothy Gedge, the unarguable strength of it, the power and the glory of it" (p. 107)), he does not tell the whole truth. For all his insights and instincts, he cannot see as deeply into human nature as he needs to because he lacks the very qualities – compassion and selflessness – that his ruthless invasions of other people's worlds prove to be missing in the community as a whole. His vision, incorrigibly cynical and desperately self-centered, is not Trevor's.

To dramatize his counterpointing faith in compassion and connection, Trevor chooses a relatively minor character, Lavinia Featherston. Lavinia's interest in Timothy is sparked in part by the knowledge that she cannot have a son of her own, and her conclusions about him are played off against her husband's view that Timothy's existence can be explained only by admitting that "God permitted chance" (p. 210). For Lavinia, to see Timothy that way is just as misleading as to take Kate's position, that he is inhabited by devils. In Lavinia's essentially humanistic view, Timothy's life can be explained in human terms only; it is a matter of human responsibility, as she considers in this crucial moment near the end of the novel:

After her long wakefulness in the night there was no escaping that thought, there was no escaping the suggestion of a pattern: the son who had not been born to her was nevertheless there for her. Believing still that the catastrophe had been caused by other people and the actions of other people, believing it as firmly as Kate believed that it had been caused by devils and Quentin that it was part of God's mystery, Lavinia saw a spark in the gloom. It was she, it seemed, not Quentin, who might somehow blow hope into hopelessness. It was she who one day, in the rectory or the garden, might penetrate the shell that out of necessity had grown. As she changed the water in her washing-up bowl, the feeling of a pattern more securely possessed her, the feeling of events happening and being linked, the feeling that her wakeful nights and her edginess over her lost child had not been without an outcome. Compassion came less easily to her than it did to her husband. She could in no way be glad that Timothy Gedge would come regularly to the rectory: that prospect was grim. Yet she felt, unable to help herself, a certain irrational joyfulness, as though an end and a beginning had been reached at the same time. You could not live without hope, some part of her woman's intuition told her: while a future was left you must not.

(p. 219)

Based on an intuitive sense of hope that counters Timothy's intuitive sense of corruption, Lavinia's belief that she might be able to rescue Timothy from the bleak future foreseen for him by her husband, that she might be able to make a useful, compassionate connection with this disturbed boy from an utterly alien social world, grows out of her conviction that Timothy's situation is the responsibility of people, not God, not Satan. Timothy himself cannot see this because his position in the class system has forced him to view human relationships – and his own life – in terms of competition and exploitation; Quentin cannot see it because of his religious beliefs.

Lavinia does not, however, get the last word in this novel. As always, Trevor works hard to discourage any reading of the book as an essentially optimistic assessment of human possibility in the contemporary world.[3] After Lavinia's epiphany, the narrative returns to Timothy himself as he wanders through Dynmouth observing the opening of the amusement park for the Easter holidays. (The use of Easter weekend for the novel's setting exemplifies the way Trevor often straddles the line between assertion and qualification; the idea of Easter can be seen as underscoring Lavinia's modest hopes of resurrecting Timothy, but from the ironic point of view that is never entirely absent from the novel, it mocks the possibility of any meaningful regeneration in Dynmouth.) Timothy has latched on to a new illusion about his life – that he is the son of Miss Lavant and Dr Greenslade, a much more romantic union than the one that actually produced him. The illusion is, of course, pathetic, and its pathos qualifies both Timothy's sense of general optimism at the end of the novel, and, by extension, Lavinia's. The book ends with a passage that leans decidedly toward irony:

> He had said to the clergyman that opportunity wouldn't knock, but you never knew and you definitely had to keep your spirits up or you'd go to the wall. One minute you discovered you could do a falsetto, the next that there was a reason why a woman had given you a sweet. Everything was waiting for you; for a start you could get money left to you in a will. He smiled at the old-age pensioner and wagged his head. 'Really good,' he said, referring to the voice of Petula Clark.
>
> The old-age pensioner could not hear it, but for everyone else it continued to throb with the promise of its message, drifting over Dynmouth on the breeze that blew gently from the sea.
>
> 'How can you lose?' sang Petula Clark. 'Things will be great.'
>
> (pp. 221–2)

Despite its relatively small canvas – one has to go back to *The Old Boys* or *A Standard of Behaviour* to find a Trevor novel of comparable brevity – *The Children of Dynmouth* has the feel of a much fuller book, partly because it is structured around so many centers of consciousness, and partly because of the density of Trevor's characterization, including that of minor figures. Moreover, Trevor's technique of fine-tuning the narrative voice to reflect the sensibility of whatever character is functioning as the center of consciousness in a given scene significantly advances and deepens characterization; with the exception of the opening panoramic description of Dynmouth, the narration of almost every passage in the book is colored by one character or another.

Another method of characterization common to Trevor's fiction, especially from the middle novels on – the shifting of narrative focus between surface events seen through a character's eyes and the memories that those events provoke – is extremely effective in *The Children of Dynmouth*. (This technique owes something to the work of Virginia Woolf, specifically to what she once referred to as her method of digging caves behind her characters.[4]) In this scene in which Stephen remembers the day he was summoned to the headmaster's office to be told by his father that his mother has died, Trevor relies on this narrative strategy to convey both the intensity of Stephen's attachment to his mother and the emotional incompatability between Stephen and his father:

> 'Died?' he whispered.
> His father was standing beside him, holding him.
> 'It's all right, Stephen,' he said, but it wasn't all right and the other two in the room knew it wasn't either. It was unbelievable, it was something that could not be true. He felt the tears on his face, a wetness that came warmly and then was chill. He struggled, as he often did in nightmares, trying to reach a surface, struggling to wake up from horror.
> 'You must be brave, old chap,' the Craw said again.
> She had a way of comforting, holding you differently from the way his father was holding him now. There was the softness of her hands, and her black hair, and a faint scent of perfume. 'Eau de Cologne,' she said. She smiled at him, her eyes lost behind sun-glasses.
> The Craw was no longer in the room. His father had a handkerchief in his hand. Stephen wept again, closing his eyes. He felt the handkerchief on his face, wiping away the tears. His father was murmuring but he couldn't hear what he was saying.
> He couldn't prevent himself from seeing her. She stood by the edge of the sea, a rust-coloured corduroy coat pulled tightly around her; he could see her breath on the icy air. He watched her making drop-scones in the kitchen of Primrose Cottage.
> Mrs Craw came in with a cup of chocolate, with the Craw behind her, carrying a tray of tea things. They didn't say anything. The Craw put the tray on the desk, and Mrs Craw poured a cup of tea for his father. They both went away again.
> 'Try and drink your chocolate,' his father said. A skin had

already formed on the surface. 'Disgusting!' he used to cry when she brought him chocolate in bed, and she'd laugh because it was a joke, because he was only pretending to be cross.

He drank the chocolate. His father repeated that it would be better if he remained in the school rather than return to Primrose Cottage. 'I'm sorry to be so little help,' his father said.

(pp. 44–5)

Although Graham Greene's Brighton may seem to be Dynmouth's nearest literary neighbor, it is perhaps more instructive to remember that Dynmouth is located squarely in the Wessex of Thomas Hardy's novels and stories. Hardy once said that pain and suffering "shall be kept down to a minimum by loving-kindness," but only when "the mighty necessitating forces . . . happen to be in equilibrium, which may or may not be often."[5] Trevor's view of the human condition is similar, but not quite so dark. His faith in compassion and connection, close relatives to Hardy's "loving-kindness," is certainly qualified, but Trevor's irony is less suffocating than the Hardyesque sense of doom that pervades the haunted heights and stunted villages of Wessex. In Trevor's world, there are no "mighty necessitating forces" to contend with, nor to blame for human suffering and unhappiness. As Lavinia Featherston says, catastrophes are "caused by other people and the actions of other people," and for that reason, some kind of redemption, brought about by the compassion of other people, is always at least possible.

OTHER PEOPLE'S WORLDS

Trevor's novels tend to rely on incongruous confrontations – Septimus Tuam worming his way into the middle-class suburban life of Eve Bolsover, Mrs Eckdorf dropping out of the sky into the seedy, decaying world of O'Neill's Hotel in Dublin, Miss Gomez preaching the gospel of forgiveness and compassion in the wasteland of Crow Street, Elizabeth Aidallbery finding herself caught up in the radically different lives of the three women with whom she is confined in the Cheltenham Street Women's Hospital, Timothy Gedge disturbing with his pathetic ambitions

74

and class-bound resentments the peace of Dynmouth's more privileged citizens. In *Other People's Worlds*, this narrative strategy is taken to its most accomplished limits, governing not just certain scenes or characters, but defining the shape of the novel as a whole, and informing everything from the arrangement and titles of chapters ("Julia's," "Francis's," "Doris's," "Julia in Francis's," "Doris in Julia's," "Julia in Doris's") to the most minute detail.

The opening scenes of the novel demonstrate how this method of structuring the narrative around confrontation and juxtaposition produces a subtle interplay – perfectly appropriate to Trevor's vision – between statement and qualification, sympathy and irony, assertion and doubt. The first few pages of the book are almost wholly introspective (like the opening of *Elizabeth Alone*), focusing on the romantic feelings of Julia Ferndale, a 47-year-old widow living a life of quiet if somewhat shabby gentility in the tranquil Gloucestershire village of Stone St Martin, for Francis Tyte, a 33-year-old part-time actor to whom she has recently become engaged. This highly subjective passage is immediately followed by a section in which Julia's mother, the elderly, sharp-minded Mrs Anstey, wrestles with her own deeply instinctive doubts about Francis's character; the juxtaposition of the two scenes hints at both Julia's vulnerability and Francis's capacity for treachery. But doubts about Julia and Francis are planted even before this, by means of a different kind of juxtaposition. In the opening passage, Julia is thinking about Francis while running some errands in preparation for a party that she is giving later to introduce Francis to some of her friends.[6] One of those errands takes her to the beauty salon, where her fantasies about her future with Francis are ironically undermined by the seemingly idle conversation of her hairdresser, a young, working-class woman about to marry a man inauspiciously named Nevil Clapp, whose past is shady if not downright criminal. The ironic implications of the suggested parallel with Julia's and Francis's relationship are advanced a few pages later in the section revealing Mrs Anstey's doubts about Francis, and then further in the party scene when Julia, in an effort to bring her mother into a polite conversation, mentions the hairdresser:

'Diane has found herself the worst possible boyfriend. Nevil Clapp.'

Mrs Anstey nodded. By all accounts, the little hairdresser had indeed made a preposterous choice and if a marriage took place she would discover her mistake within a week. Yet what girl alive would listen to her parents when they warned her that the boy she loved would one day seek to entice her into the realm of corruption?[7]

Mrs Anstey obviously has more on her mind here than the hairdresser and Nevil; her thoughts both suggest the *naïveté* of Julia's perception of Francis, and forecast the demise of that relationship.

The relationship between Julia and Francis is one of the most incongruous of the many unhappy confrontations that occur in the novel, a false connection built on Julia's blindness to reality and Francis's perverse gift for exploiting that blindness. Ultimately, the connection – but only after it is severed – draws Julia into another confrontation with a world radically different from her tranquil, seemingly secure and morally ordered upper-middle-class life as a widow in Stone St Martin: the deranged, insecure, morally chaotic, lower-class world of Doris Smith's London. Both these confrontations have their thematic significance; Francis and Doris, predator and victim, are figures of disconnection and alienation, and Julia, through her disturbing encounters with them, is eventually forced out of her isolation and into an awareness of the necessity of compassion and connection. But these two confrontations also, like their counterparts in *The Children of Dynmouth*, have strong social implications; the barriers that Julia has to cross are constructed not of personal idiosyncrasy alone, but also of the divisive effects of a rigid social system.[8]

This is insisted on in part by the setting of the novel. Placid, pastoral descriptions of Stone St Martin and Julia's residence there, Swan House, are played against relentlessly bleak descriptions of the various undersides of London life, familiar territory for the author of *Miss Gomez and the Brethren*. When, for example, Doris's 12-year-old daughter Joy stops off at the Rialto Café on her way home from school, her thoughts are complemented by a conversation at a nearby table about the making of pornographic films, a spatial juxtaposition that portrays a society as far as possible from the quiet, shaded garden of Swan House, and that also subtly suggests a future for Joy at least as bleak as that which lies ahead of Timothy Gedge:

The middle-aged couple had begun to argue, which pleased Joy because that was something to listen to. The woman emphasized the points she was making by striking the surface of the table with a ketchup container, a roundish plastic object like a large tomato. 'She came back in a shocking state,' she said. 'Nothing that wasn't torn.' Joy couldn't hear the man's reply, and then the woman said, 'Of course you bloody had the camera going.'

Joy was in 3B at Tite Street Comprehensive, where the current fashion was starting fires. She belonged to a group, the fans of a pop band called The Insane; the other group in the class were supporters of Fulham Football Club. A fire had been started in a French period that morning by one of the Insane fans, and a second one during the lunch-hour by the Fulham supporters. A month ago paint-guns had been all the rage, but everyone was sick of them now.

The woman brought the Tizer and the chips, fewer chips than usual, Joy noticed. 'No bloody way,' the man at the next table protested angrily. 'No way you can call them blue.'

(p. 63)

In a novel so dependent on juxtaposition and parallelism, there can be few insignificant coincidences. And it is certainly no meaningless accident that just after Joy leaves the Rialto Café, her head full of the horrors of her school and the perverse conversation of her fellow-diners, she sees Francis, her father. Nor is it mere chance that Francis should be at that moment escorting into a pub the actress, Susanna Music, playing the part of Constance Kent in a television drama in which Francis has a small role. The story of Constance Kent, a nineteenth-century adolescent accused of butchering her infant brother in a fit of revengeful rage against her father, has a bearing on all the major characters in the novel, including Joy. First mentioned in passing in *The Children of Dynmouth*, this gothic tale is one of the novel's most effective means of forging and revealing connections between characters; it is worked in and out of the narrative, generating a complex series of thematically relevant echoes and parallels while dispensing an appropriately unsettling atmosphere of emotional imbalance and malice.

It first surfaces, with characteristic suggestiveness, in Mrs Anstey's consciousness, just after the party described in the opening chapter:

She forced herself to smile around the table and then listened when the talk turned to the Victorian murder case in which Francis was to play a part. He was to be an under-gardener, and while he spoke she endeavoured to fill her mind with the scenes he colourfully described. Someone called Constance Kent it was all about, an adolescent girl who had cut a child's throat.

(p. 30)

The sinister implications set up here by association – Francis has been doing the gardening at Swan House, and he will later play a very real if indirect role in a twentieth-century murder, that of his wife in Folkestone – are advanced at the end of the first chapter when Francis thinks again about Constance Kent while removing the facial make-up that he always wears, and then a few pages later in a striking fantasy that suggests, among other things, Julia's potential to be one of his victims:

Poor violent creature, not to be allowed to remain in the twilight of her death but to end up so trivially on the television screen, neither real nor unreal. In a limbo somewhere she was no doubt a weeping ghost, and out of sympathy, or just for fun, Francis decorated her adolescent nakedness with Julia Ferndale's jewellery. The little sapphires gleamed on her pale white skin, the dragon brooch was miraculously suspended, the seed-pearl necklace fell coolly from her neck. He smiled as he lay there, considering the image extraordinary.

(pp. 41–2)

As the novel develops, Francis increasingly identifies with Constance, seeing himself as a victim and therefore entitled to some kind of revenge. ("All I'm saying," Doris tells Julia at one point, "is poor Francis was made for suffering, like the Kent girl was" (p. 167).) Constance's story specifically inspires a vivid fantasy on Francis's part of beating his wife to death, an act that Doris actually commits. Doris is also associated more directly with the Constance Kent story. Both hated their step-mothers (Doris left home, in fact, after her father remarried), both consider themselves victimized by injustice, both strike out in desperate, deranged revenge, Constance against her brother, Doris against Francis's wife. The morning that Doris sets out for Folkestone, where Francis's wife lives, her thoughts keep returning to a perception of Constance as a suffering victim – "the story of poor little Constance Kent, who had suffered as he [Francis] had and as she had herself" (p. 220).

The Constance Kent story also plays a significant part in the book's final assertion, and qualification, of the principle of compassion and connection. The television drama made out of the story is finally broadcast, and most of the characters in the novel see it. In one sense, this event serves as an ironic comment on the possibility of connection; the link that it forms between the characters who watch the program – everyone from the people in Stone St Martin who came to Julia's party to Doris Smith's fellow-employees in the shoeshop and Francis's parents in their nursing home in Hampton Wick – is artificial and temporary. On the other hand, it is the Constance Kent story, watched by Julia at Swan House, that sparks Julia's commitment to trying to redeem Joy. The television drama forces Julia to recognize both the extent to which Joy, like Constance Kent, has been a "victim of other people's worlds," and her own responsibility, as a human being necessarily caught up in a web of human connections, to exercise compassion:

> An unbalanced girl revenged herself on the television screen, but it was not her story which had a point to make in the bow-windowed drawing-room of Swan House. . . . The act of murder that was premeditated in the steamy Victorian household had been carried into the child's life, inspired by her father, perpetrated by her mother. The child was the victim of other people's worlds and other people's drama, caught up in horror because she happened to be there. . . . The child would grow into adolescence and womanhood, pinning the fragments together: her mother and her father, victim and predator, truth and illusion. It was too late to change Francis's fate, or Doris's, or the debt-collector's or the dressmaker's. . . . It was the child's story that mattered.
>
> (p. 242)

In terms of the authenticity of this novel's vision of alienation and disconnection, it is Francis's story that matters. A social predator and compulsive purveyor of illusion, Francis represents the culmination in Trevor's fiction of the deceiving and self-deceived con-man, the exploiter of connection and compassion –

a line stretching from Basil Jaraby in *The Old Boys* to Studdy in *The Boarding-House*, Septimus Tuam in *The Love Department*, Morrissey in *Mrs Eckdorf in O'Neill's Hotel*, Mr Maloney in *Elizabeth Alone*, and Timothy Gedge in *The Children of Dynmouth*. Of all these characters, Francis is the most dramatically realized and psychologically convincing. The dramatic impact of his character is heightened by the calculatedly gradual revelation of the full scope of his treachery and depravity, beginning with the subtly sinister overtones of the scene in the first chapter in which he is observed removing his make-up and leading up to the scene, about a third of the way through the book, in which he cruises the Piccadilly Circus area for homosexuals. The psychological realism of his character depends in part on Trevor's manipulation of narrative voice in scenes in which Francis is the center of consciousness; in the following three passages, for instance – the first describing Francis's decision not to tell Julia the truth about his marriage to the dressmaker in Folkestone, the second his thoughts about being a father, and the third his feelings about abandoning Doris and Joy – the narrative voice quietly but effectively discloses the way that Francis's distorted mind works:

> But the marriage itself now belonged in the past, and Francis saw no reason to burden the women of Swan House with it. To have done so would have sounded as out-of-place in their drawing-room as regaling them with the fact that a girl in a department store had once borne a child of his, or with various other facts about himself.
>
> (pp. 36–7)

> He found it hard to understand why he had wished, so many years ago, to watch this shop girl becoming pregnant. All he certainly knew was that when the experience of fathering a child had come about it had been only another disappointment.
>
> (p. 41)

> He would never again see her or her child. She loved him, as the dressmaker had, and the doctor's wife, as Julia Ferndale did. The ill fortune in her life had been cheered by this love; the memory of it would be a comfort for her in the future.
>
> (p. 130)

Francis's self-interest and powers of rationalization are obvious in all three passages, especially the last. But the banal, understated, non-incriminating phrases employed by the narrator – "saw no reason to burden the women," "would have sounded . . . out-of-place in their drawing-room," "to watch this shop girl becoming pregnant," "The ill fortune in her life" – also convey his more thematically significant lack of moral judgment, his inability, or unwillingness, to take into account the effects of his actions on other people and their worlds.

The narrative voice is also shaded at times to develop sympathy for Francis, or at least encourage some ambiguity in the reader's response to him.[9] Like most central figures in Trevor's novels, Francis is perceived from various points of view, including his own. Julia, after Francis has left her in Italy, tends to see him as motivated principally by cruelty and the need to strike out against the social classes above him: "Of course it was out of cruelty that he had bigamously married her, of course it was to mock her and insult her. He hated the kind of person she was; he had begun to revenge himself from the first moment he'd laid eyes on her" (p. 158). Doris, befogged by alcohol and an incorrigible romanticism, excuses Francis's behavior by blaming his unfortunate childhood experience with a homosexual debt-collector who was a lodger in his parents's house. The truth of Francis's character lies not so much in the middle of these two positions – Francis as victimizer, Francis as victim – as along a path moving back and forth between them, a route that Trevor traces by manipulating the reader's attitude toward Francis between repulsion and sympathy, rejection and understanding. Even the scene in which Francis is at his most repugnant – when he picks up a homosexual near Piccadilly Circus – concludes with a subjective description designed to generate some sympathy for him: "When it was over Francis walked away from the garage with the money the man had given him. Tears oozed from the corners of his eyes, leaving tiny tracks in his make-up, causing his face to seem older. He wished he didn't always cry" (p. 86). And the lengthy introspective passage describing Francis's childhood that follows this scene, although by no means meant to encourage the easy psychologizing that blinds Doris to the genuine malice in Francis, suggests the extent to which he is victim as well as victimizer:

With the colourful regiments spread out on the table kept

specially for war games, the same words were always whispered, the same passion entered the debt-collector's eyes. Among the marching soldiers the deception and the treachery increased, becoming as much part of everything as the acts the debt-collector taught him. School, and the friends there might have been there, became absurd. His mother and his father seemed like two bothersome old mice, filling the sitting-room with fustiness. . . . He was ashamed, he explained to the doctor's wife, to stand in the same room as his parents; but all the doctor's wife had done was to take advantage of him also. In the end the debt-collector had paid him.

(p. 89)

If Francis and Doris embody the morally corrosive values of exploitation and alienation – all the human relationships that both of them establish are broken or incomplete, and even Doris's conversation consists chiefly of fragments that she does not understand and that are misinterpreted by her listeners – it is in the development of Julia's character from social isolation to some kind of engagement with other people's worlds that Trevor dramatizes his vision of the counterpointing need for compassion and connection. Just after Doris and Joy visit her at Swan House, following her return from Italy, Julia becomes aware of being dragged into a vast, intricate, and, at this point, terrifying web of connections lying beyond her deliberately confined life in Stone St Martin:

In the train there'd be the journey to the bar, and the child staring out at the passing landscape, not wanting to be tattooed. In Folkestone there was a harmless dressmaker whose misfortune it had been to meet Francis Tyte on the sea-front. In other parts of England there were other people, who shuddered when they recalled his name. In Hampton Wick the confusion was as he wished it to be.

When he had spent the money her jewellery raised, his letter with its German stamp would arrive. He would exact his self-allocated due as he always had from the people he came across, but it wasn't that that concerned Julia now. For the second time that summer a woman's intuition nagged uncomfortably in Swan House: the pattern she had once been unable to discern, not even then being aware of the people it involved, spread itself chillingly through her. Connections suddenly were everywhere, an ugly sense crept out of hiding.

(p. 189)

Despite Julia's powerful, solipsistic fear of another disasterous connection with the world outside Swan House, the inescapable link between Julia and Doris eventually forces her to revise her perception of her own life, to see it as resting on a privileged and morally condemnable innocence. Not long after meeting with Doris and Joy, she writes in her diary: "*I have lived too long among flowerbeds, I move from room to room of my doll's house. . . . I pray to my childhood God, yet in this pretty town my life has been less real than other people's*" (p. 190). Later, in a lengthy conversation with Father Lavin – similar in function and effect to the talk between Elizabeth and Miss Samson near the end of *Elizabeth Alone* – Julia tells the priest about the tragic lives of Doris and Joy, and about several other events, such as the clubbing to death of some pentecostal missionaries, that have shaken her faith in her own life and religious values. And when Father Lavin tells her that she is "making connections that are not there," Julia argues that "surely God's creatures are all connected," and adds: "Those missionaries died on the hard earth of their compound, and Stone St Martin nestles among the lazy wolds of Gloucestershire. How can the destruction of Doris Smith belong in the same world as the contentment of the people who came that night to have drinks on our lawn?" (p. 197).

The answer is, as Julia fully realizes by the end of the novel, that all these things are connected, that the world of other people's pain cannot be fenced off, and human beings have, therefore, a responsibility to extend themselves with compassion. Julia's commitment to rescuing Joy from the destructive future that seems to await her grows out of this humanistic attitude. And like Lavinia Featherston's decision to help Timothy Gedge, it generates in Julia a new sense of meaning and purpose, along with an understanding that the old ways of her life are no longer morally valid.[10] The novel concludes on this note, and on an image of renewal and regeneration:

> She washed. She brushed her teeth. She slipped her clothes from her, reflecting that company law and title deeds had failed her already. Her silenced mind would not accept the strictures she imposed; some part of her insisted that she might as well not

exist if she ceased to wonder, she couldn't pack God and Francis Tyte away. All she completely knew was that the niceness of her world was not entirely without purpose . . .

She put her nightdress on and got into bed, gazing for a while into the darkness before she slept. The child should not have been born but the child was there, her chapped face and plastic-rimmed spectacles. She was there in the garden and the house, while time went on and the seasons unfussily changed. Leaves from the tulip tree floated away on the river, in spring there were mornings of sunshine.

(p. 243)

During a conversation in which Doris tells Julia about Uncle Manchester, an ailing relative that Francis has invented as an excuse not to stay with Doris, Julia thinks about Francis's powers of creativity: "the invention of this man belonged in the same grey limbo as the process of going through a marriage ceremony. There were the same elaborations of pretending, with truth and lies insidiously mixed and an outcome full of other people's pain" (p. 180). Francis has an extraordinary imagination, but it is unreined, not tied to any moral vision or principles, a power that mixes truth and lies easily.[11] Trevor has given this undisciplined ability to other characters – Miss Gomez, Mrs Eckdorf, Septimus Tuam, Timothy Gedge – and they are all unbalanced and a little dangerous.

This has revealing implications for Trevor's view of the novelist. As he said in the interview quoted at the beginning of this chapter, Trevor is not an autobiographical novelist, but a writer working primarily out of a "curiosity about situations and people." This attitude tends to turn Trevor away from solipsistic or metafictional preoccupations, and toward a view of the writer as necessarily and morally engaged with the society in which he lives. It is only Francis – and characters like him, living in a self-spun fantasy world – who can say, "Make-belief is all we have" (p. 68).

84

5

"SUCH TALES OF WOE":
The Short Stories

Three years after the appearance of his second novel, *The Old Boys*, Trevor published his first collection of short stories, *The Day We Got Drunk on Cake* (1967). Like *The Old Boys*, this book seemed more the work of an experienced, accomplished author than the efforts of a relative novice. Its twelve stories are remarkably consistent in quality, and many of the formal characteristics of *The Old Boys* – the precise diction, the use of concrete, extremely suggestive details, the sparse, economical plots and sub-plots constructed around parallelism and juxtaposition, the carefully modulated ironies – prove at least as effective in these stories as they are in the novel.

The promise of *The Day We Got Drunk on Cake* has more than been fulfilled. Over the course of two decades, Trevor has published six volumes of short stories, and although the six-dozen stories in these collections range widely in terms of subject-matter and thematic concerns, and employ a broad variety of styles and story-telling modes, they are characterized by a consistently impressive level of craftsmanship and – at their best – by an intensity and complexity that place Trevor in the very first rank of contemporary short-story writers. Indeed, it is possible to argue that the short story, with its demands for nuance and economy, for suggestiveness and precision, is the form most amenable to Trevor's literary sensibility.[1]

Trevor's stories fall somewhere between the radical experimentation of modernists like Joyce and Woolf and the relative conservatism of more conventional tale-tellers like Kipling in England and Frank O'Connor in Ireland. One way to categorize them is as "free stories," a term coined by Trevor's fellow Anglo-Irish writer Elizabeth Bowen.[2] Although free stories tend to play down plot, they do not go so far as to replace anecdotal narrative structures with essentially symbolic ones (as some of Joyce's stories do),[3] nor are they mainly interested in interrogating such fundamental fictional concepts as character and setting (as do many of the stories of Woolf and Beckett). Instead, the free story, perhaps best exemplified in the work of Bowen and V. S. Pritchett, is committed to exploring human character with psychological authenticity and Chekhovian subtlety – relying largely on suggestion, irony, and cinematic juxtaposition to do so – and in anchoring its characters in meaningful social realities.

Although some of Trevor's stories are slightly more traditional than many free stories, his short fiction is essentially committed to this notion of what the short story can do.[4] For one thing, his stories depend on highly realistic surfaces that also work to suggest underlying moral and psychological complexities. Trevor's characteristic handling of narrative voice, observed in his novels, contributes significantly to this effect. By negotiating between a relatively distant, neutral tone and one highly colored by the qualities of certain characters, Trevor's narrators are able both to present a relatively objective surface and to indicate by suggestion subjective psychological and emotional currents running beneath it. This flexible narrative voice needs to be distinguished from the scrupulously dispassionate voice that governs most of Joyce's stories in *Dubliners*, discouraging subjective identification with any character. It also differentiates Trevor's stories from the work of contemporary "minimalist" writers like Raymond Carver and Ann Beattie, whose narrators tend to be more one-dimensionally flat and limited.[5]

The moral vision behind Trevor's short stories tends to be somewhat darker than that which informs his novels. The faith in compassion and connection that is affirmed, albeit with qualification, at the end of novels like *Elizabeth Alone*, *The Children of Dynmouth*, and *Other People's Worlds* is largely absent from the stories. Characters in them tend to be not only alienated and disconnected, but also rarely able to discover the means to break out of their social and moral estrangement, or to overcome the crippling illusions with which they mask their inadequacies.[6] Attempts at connection usually go astray or fail altogether; characters are either victims or victimizers, "clinging to the periphery of life,'' as one of them puts it,[7] and they stay that way.

The most effective objective correlative that Trevor employs for this bleak vision is the corruption or destruction of love. More than half of Trevor's stories take love as their principal subject, almost always in ways that dramatize alienation and disconnection: marriages dissolved or coming apart ("Access to the Children," "Angels at the Ritz"), love displaced by casual sexual relations ("Office Romances," "The Forty-Seventh Saturday"), romance worn down and defeated by time and circumstances ("The Day We Got Drunk on Cake," "Lovers of Their Time"). Trevor's interest in middle-class marriages, evident in novels like *The Love Department* and *Elizabeth Alone*, and comparable to some of John Updike's writing, is especially manifest in a number of stories concerned with divorce and its effects.[8]

These stories about love and marriage tend to focus on the losers – sometimes the man ("Access to the Children"), sometimes the woman ("Angels at the Ritz"), sometimes the children ("Mrs Silly"). As such, they exemplify a tendency in many of Trevor's stories – in keeping with the tradition of the free story – to dramatize their thematic concerns through character. Trevor's stories are full of alienated, lonely people: middle-aged women living lives of quiet desperation in London bed-sitters; shy, repressed bachelors incapable of love or sexual relationships; the elderly; the abandoned; the eccentric. Mr Mileson, a bachelor in a story entitled "A Meeting in Middle Age," is typical: "He would leave little behind, he thought. He would die and there would be the things in the room, rather a number of useless things with sentimental value only. Ornaments and ferns. Reproductions of paintings. A set of eggs, birds' eggs he had collected as a boy. They would pile all the junk together and probably try to burn it.''[9]

In Trevor's first three volumes of stories – *The Day We Got Drunk on Cake*, *The Ballroom of Romance* (1972), and *Angels at the Ritz* (1975) – these characters exist in worlds more or less detached from historical or political realities. Whatever past is evoked is private rather than public, psychological rather than political. But with *Lovers of Their Time* (1978) and the two collections of stories that follow it – *Beyond the Pale* (1981) and *The News from Ireland* (1986) – Trevor's stories increasingly evidence a political and historical consciousness; characters are portrayed as victims specifically of history, caught in the grip of forces over which they have little or no control.[10] Ireland provides the most dramatic stage for the working out of this view, and it is no accident that some of Trevor's most psychologically convincing stories have to do with Ireland, particularly with the sectarian violence in contemporary Ulster.

Although Trevor's stories are, on the whole, remarkably consistent in terms of their level of accomplishment and effectiveness, there are flaws that need to be pointed out, if only to call attention to the risks that these kinds of stories entail. Characterization is occasionally thin, either because a story is not large enough to accommodate all that Trevor wants to put in it, or because character is sacrificed to thematic concerns.[11] In a story entitled "Torridge," for example, Trevor sets up a confrontation between three comfortable middle-class families and a man who was once, in the public-school days of the three husbands, the butt of many schoolboy jokes. The sudden appearance of this man, his admission that he is a homosexual, and his revelations about the homosexual nature of all their schoolboy experiences is intended, like the words of most of Trevor's truth-tellers, to jolt his listeners into facing a reality buried beneath the apparently secure surface of their lives. Unfortunately, the effect is largely lost because there are too many characters for Trevor to be able to develop a significant interest in any one or two of them. In a late story entitled "Butterflies," a potentially provocative development of character is overwhelmed by the impulse to get across a moral point. The story opens with a strong difference of opinion between a man and his wife over a local political issue, but the question of how this public matter might affect the precarious balance of a marriage is abandoned for the more reductively didactic question raised by the issue itself: whether a residential community of well-to-do people should allow a home for mentally disturbed women to be set up in their midst.

These kinds of failings are, however, remarkably rare, and do not detract seriously from the considerable achievement of Trevor's short stories as a whole, an achievement that the rest of this chapter will attempt to measure by examining a selection of the most representative and accomplished of them.

"The Table," the first story in Trevor's first collection of stories, presents – in microcosmic form – many of the situations and concerns that run through Trevor's novels: a confrontation between people from different classes, a plot that tracks the attempt of one character to break out of a solipsistic existence and establish some connection with a world beyond his own, and a climactic scene in which one character takes on the role of truth-teller. On one side is Mr Jeffs, very much a figure of alienation – a bachelor whose life is devoted only to his antiques business, and a Jew; on the other are the Hammonds, a well-off middle-class couple considerably higher up the social ladder than Mr Jeffs. In the process of buying a table from the Hammonds, Mr Jeffs begins to suspect that Mr Hammond is carrying on an adulterous relationship with a young woman named Mrs Youghal, and this provokes him to the uncharacteristically selfless action of revealing his suspicions to Mrs Hammond in an attempt to help her see the truth about her marriage. But there is no illumination, no real connection established; the news stuns Mrs Hammond into silence, and Mr Jeffs is left with self-condemnation as his only reward. The story ends with an epiphany that is thoroughly Joycean in its disillusionment and in its acceptance of alienation as a necessary condition:

> Mr Jeffs drove on, aware of a sadness but aware as well that his mind was slowly emptying itself of Mrs Hammond and her husband and the beautiful Mrs Youghal. 'I cook my own food,' said Mr Jeffs aloud. 'I am a good trader, and I do not bother anyone.' He had no right to hope that he might have offered comfort. He had no business to take such things upon himself, to imagine that a passage of sympathy might have developed between himself and Mrs Hammond.
>
> 'I cook my own food,' said Mr Jeffs again. 'I do not bother anyone.' He drove in silence after that, thinking of nothing at all. The chill of sadness left him, and the mistake he had made appeared to him as a fact that could not be remedied. He noticed that dusk was falling; and he returned to the house where he had never lit a fire, where the furniture loomed and did not smile at him, where nobody wept and nobody told a lie.
>
> (p. 23)

"The Table" also demonstrates Trevor's ability, so crucial to the free story, to create a surface as strongly suggestive as it is fully realized. In the following passage, for example, both the social gap between Mr Jeffs and the Hammonds and the nature of Mr Jeffs's character are conveyed with the efficiency demanded of this type of short story:

> 'I've been clever,' said Mrs Hammond to her husband. 'I have sold the console table to a little man called Mr Jeffs whom Ursula and I at first mistook for a window-cleaner.' Mr Jeffs put a chalk mark on the table and made a note of it in a notebook. He sat in the kitchen of his large house, eating kippers that he had cooked in a plastic bag. His jaws moved slowly and slightly, pulping the fish as a machine might.
>
> (pp. 9–10)

Mrs Hammond's description of Mr Jeffs as "a little man" and her amused reference to the mistake made about his identity pinpoint precisely the class and ethnic attitudes that the story is concerned with. The sudden, cinematic shift to Mr Jeffs in his house, and especially the nicely observed detail about the kippers cooked in a plastic bag, dramatically define the distance between the two worlds of the story. And finally, the last image on the one hand suggests the stereotypical view of Jews as aggressive – the kind of assumption that Mrs Hammond takes as truth – and on the other functions ironically, given Mr Jeffs's true status as an alienated victim.

Both *The Old Boys* and "The General's Day," the second story in *The Day We Got Drunk on Cake*, focus on the elderly, and both end darkly. But the strong strain of comedy that takes some of the edge off the essentially tragic shape of *The Old Boys* is much less in evidence in "The General's Day." The story has its comic moments, including scenes dependent on the same kind of linguistic humor found in *The Old Boys*, but it is much more relentlessly fixed on its vision of alienation than is the novel.

The story is structured around a series of attempts by the protagonist, a lonely retired general named Suffolk, to make connections, to reach out, as Mr Jeffs tries to do in "The Table," beyond the confines of his solipsistic world. No connections are made, however; each attempt ends in a cruel, pathetic rejection: the young boy Basil says he cannot accompany General Suffolk to the movies, but later is seen there by the General; the General's supposed friend Mr Frobisher will not come out to meet him, and the General overhears him tell his wife, "Oh my dear, can't you tell him I'm out?" (p. 32); and finally a middle-aged married woman with the Dickensian name of Mrs Hope-Kingley walks abruptly away when the General tries to pick her up in a teashop. It all ends with the General in the arms, literally, of a predator, his mean-spirited cleaning-woman, Mrs Hinch, a character typical of the victimizer in Trevor's fiction, someone who sees human relationships chiefly in terms of power struggles. The story concludes with the General's arrival home, drunk, at the end of his disappointing day, and with a devastatingly bleak moment of self-understanding:

> The General laughed. Clumsily he slapped her broad buttocks. She screamed shrilly, enjoying the position she now held over him. 'Dirty old General! Hinchie won't carry her beauty home unless he's a good boy tonight.' She laughed her cackling laugh and the General joined in it. He dawdled a bit, and losing her patience Mrs Hinch pushed him roughly in front of her. He fell, and in picking him up she came upon his wallet and skilfully extracted two pounds ten. 'General would fancy his Hinchie tonight,' she said, shrieking merrily at the thought. But the General was silent now, seeming almost asleep as he walked. His face was gaunt and thin, with little patches of red. 'I could live for twenty years,' he whispered. 'My God Almighty, I could live for twenty years.' Tears spread on his cheeks. 'Lor' love a duck!' cried Mrs Hinch; and leaning on the arm of this stout woman the hero of Roeux and Monchy-le-Preux stumbled the last few yards to his cottage.
>
> (pp. 43–4)

The effect of this epiphany, and of the story as a whole, depend significantly on Trevor's ability to maintain sympathy for the General, even when, as in the teashop scene, he acts badly. This is where Trevor's manipulation of narrative voice becomes crucial. In the following passage, for example, the narrator's voice is distinctly colored by the highly formal, somewhat arch tone of the General's speech, generating sympathy for the General by contrasting his relatively refined sensibility, felt in the narrative tone, with the coarseness of the world in which the General finds himself forced to live:

A man carrying a coil of garden hose tripped and fell across his path. This man, a week-end visitor to the district, known to the General by sight and disliked by him, uttered as he dropped to the ground a series of expletives of a blasphemous and violent nature. The General, since the man's weight lay on his shoes, stooped to assist him. 'Oh, buzz off,' ordered the man, his face close to the General's. So the General left him, conscious not so much of his dismissal as of the form of words it had taken.

(p. 31)

The intimacy between the narrative voice and the General's character carries this scene beyond the slapstick comedy of its surface, and even beyond its status as another symbolic moment of rejection in the General's day. By embodying in its language the contrast between the General's old-world graciousness and the rude, alienating character of the man whom he tries to help, it conveys dramatically the bankruptcy of morals and manners in contemporary society, and the futility of attempts at exercising compassion and connection in such a world.

Although it looks back in setting and character to Trevor's first novel, *A Standard of Behaviour*, and ahead to the later novels and stories concerned with love and marriage, the title story of *The Day We Got Drunk on Cake* seems to represent, in formal terms, a direction that Trevor tried once and then abandoned. It is also one of the most thematically ambitious of Trevor's early stories, and one of the most successful.

Apart from the opening two paragraphs, which exhibit the same imitative, artificial tone that characterizes much of *A Standard of Behaviour* – "Garbed in a crushed tweed suit, fingering the ragged end of a tie that might well have already done a year's service about his waist, Swann de Courcey uttered a convivial obscenity in the four hundred cubic feet of air they euphemistically called my office" (p. 144) – the style of this story is extremely and uncharacteristically sparse, with an occasional trace of Hemingway in the narrative voice and dialogue that comes as close as Trevor gets to minimalist writers like Raymond Carver and Ann Beattie. The following telephone conversation, between the narrator, a young man drifting through an afternoon and evening of aimless party-going and pub-crawling, and a girl named Lucy with whom he is in love and whom he keeps calling, is typical:

'Hullo, Lucy. What are you doing?'

'What d'you mean, what am I doing? I'm standing here talking to you on the telephone.'

'I'm getting drunk with people in Soho.'

'Well, that's nice for you.'

'Is it? Wish you were here.'

Lucy would be bored by this. 'I've been reading *Adam Bede*,' she said.

'A good story.'

'Yes.'

'Have you had lunch?'

'I couldn't find anything. I had some chocolate.'

'I telephoned to see how you were.'

'I'm fine, thanks.'

'I wanted to hear your voice.'

'Oh come off it. It's just a voice.'

'Shall I tell you about it?'

'I'd rather you didn't. I don't know why.'

'Shall we meet some time?'

'I'm sure we shall.'

'I'll ring you when I'm sober.'

'Do that. I must get back to *Adam Bede*.'

'Goodbye.'

'Goodbye.'

I replaced the receiver and stood there looking down the steep stairs. Then I descended them.

'What on earth shall we do now?' Swann said. 'It's four o'clock.'

(p. 147)

That final allusion to Eliot's *Wasteland* is perfectly appropriate to "The Day We Got Drunk on Cake," a story in which fragmented relationships function as barometers of society's moral and spiritual impoverishment.[12] The narrator's apparently futile feelings for Lucy – in his last phone call, he discovers that another man is spending the night with her – are complemented by other unfulfilled relationships, in particular a rocky marriage between Margo, one of the women in the casual group of drinkers, and her husband Nigel. As the other woman in the foursome, Jo, says to the narrator at one point, "Nobody knows what to do about

anyone else'' (p. 149), a statement that goes to the heart of many
of Trevor's later stories about love.

Ultimately, "The Day We Got Drunk on Cake" ranges beyond
this portrayal of moral incongruity and meaninglessness. The
futility and absurdity experienced by the narrator throughout the
story, and embodied in the story's title, serve finally to set the
stage for the narrator's closing epiphanic reflections about the
passage of time and how it destroys passion even as it heals. It is
a moment, relatively rare in Trevor's fiction, in which the usual
ironies generated by carefully manipulated distances between
narrator and character are dispensed with in favor of a direct,
unambiguous expression that is psychologically authentic and
philosophically poignant. Its lyricism is all the more affecting,
coming at the end of a story marked by an extremely flat, colorless
prose:

> As for me, time would heal and time would cure. I knew it, and
> it was the worst thing of all. I didn't want to be cured. I wanted
> the madness of my love for Lucy to go on lurching at me from
> dreams; to mock at me from half-empty glasses; to leap at me
> unexpectedly. In time Lucy's face would fade to a pin-point; in
> time I would see her on the street and greet her with casualness,
> and sit with her over coffee, quietly discussing the flow beneath
> the bridges since last we met. Today – not even that, for
> already it was tomorrow – would slide away like all the other
> days. Not a red letter day. Not the day of my desperate
> bidding. Not the day on which the love of my life was snaffled
> away from me. I opened the front door and looked out into the
> night. It was cold and uncomforting. I liked it like that. I hated
> the moment, yet I loved it because in it I still loved Lucy.
> Deliberately I swung the door and shut away the darkness and
> drizzle. As I went back to the party the sadness of all the forget-
> ting stung me. Even already, I thought, time is at work; time
> is ticking her away; time is destroying her, killing all there was
> between us. And with time on my side I would look back on the
> day without bitterness and without emotion. I would remember
> it only as a flash on the brittle surface of nothing, as a day that
> was rather funny, as the day we got drunk on cake.
>
> (p. 159)

Although it is neither as accomplished nor as ambitious as "The

Day We Got Drunk on Cake,'' ''Raymond Bamber and Mrs Fitch'' is more representative of Trevor's short stories, in terms both of its characters and structure and of its thematic concern with the nature and necessity of illusions. The story turns on a characteristic confrontation between two very different people, both familiar figures in Trevor's fiction. Raymond Bamber is a shy, repressed, 42-year-old bachelor living a life taken up principally with furnishing his flat; in sexual matters, he is a genuine naif, like Edward Blakeston-Smith in *The Love Department*. Mrs Fitch is an outspoken, garrulous woman of the world, a contemporary Wife of Bath who, in an aggressive conversation with Raymond at a cocktail party, challenges his self-deceiving illusion that his life is as fully satisfying and meaningful as anyone else's. Like many of Trevor's truth-tellers – Mrs Eckdorf and Miss Gomez, most notably – Mrs Fitch has a highly overactive imagination, but she is able to see through illusions and pretences designed to mask disturbing truths, psychological or societal. She tells Raymond, for example, that her husband has been unfaithful to her, and that such behavior is common in their circles, information that is deeply troubling to Raymond's childish need to believe in order and fidelity and to ignore the realities of sexual desire and irrationality. She also tells him, cruelly, that most people see him as ''a grinding bore'' (p. 169).

Whether it is viewed as an attempted connection between two disparate people, or as an effort by one character to force another to face the truth about himself, this confrontation, like many such encounters in Trevor's stories, fails. Raymond is given evidence that Mrs Fitch, for all the distracted quality of her talk and appearance, cannot be dismissed as mad – ''She has a reputation,'' Raymond is told by another woman at the party, ''for getting drunk and coming out with awkward truths'' (p. 176) – but her messages cannot penetrate his defenses. The end of the story suggests that illusions, however crippling, are not so easily destroyed, and, may, in fact, be necessary for survival in a world of alienation:

Soon afterwards, Raymond left the party and walked through the autumn evening, considering everything. The air was cool on his face as he strode towards Bayswater, thinking that as he continued to live his quiet life Mrs Fitch would be attending parties that were similar to the Tamberlys', and she'd be telling the people she met there that they were grinding bores. The people might be offended, Raymond thought, if they didn't pause to think about it, if they didn't understand that everything was confused in poor Mrs Fitch's mind. And it would serve them right, he reflected, to be offended – a just reward for allowing their minds to become lazy and untidy in this modern manner. 'Orderliness,' said the voice of Nanny Wilkinson, and Raymond paused and smiled, and then walked on.

(pp. 179–80)

Not only does this passage subvert the convention of bringing a short story of this type to rest on a moment of illumination or self-understanding, but also it exemplifies some of the effects gained by Trevor's handling of narrative voice. Although the passage is undoubtedly ironic – Raymond is, after all, clinging to self-deception and self-delusion – the irony is qualified somewhat by the narrative voice, which, in its practised serenity and slightly priggish note of condescension, is extremely close to Raymond's character. And so the passage walks the line between irony and sympathy, allowing Trevor to convey simultaneously the destructive nature of illusions and the human need for them.

Characters like Raymond Bamber, General Suffolk, and Mr Jeffs are eccentrics, inhabiting the outskirts of society, and Trevor's use of such figures as lenses through which to view society is in keeping with Frank O'Connor's notions about how the story tends to work.[13] And although Trevor never fully abandons his interest in such out-of-the-way characters, in his next volume of stories, *The Ballroom of Romance*, he begins to direct his attention more toward the mainstream of society, the middle class especially, and toward love and marriage.

Both these preoccupations inform the opening story of the volume, "Access to the Children," a story substantially different from anything in *The Day We Got Drunk on Cake*. Its protagonist, Malcolmson, is a middle-aged, middle-class man who, at one time, led a comfortable, conventional family life. At the beginning of the story, however, all that is in the past – a temporary love affair with a younger woman ended Malcolmson's marriage – and the story charts Malcolmson's drift toward the edges of society and a life consumed by illusions. In many ways, Malcolmson is a fore-runner of Henry, the childhood friend of Elizabeth in *Elizabeth Alone* whose life of illusion and disappointment ends in suicide.[14]

Malcolmson is more fully and more subtly realized than is any character in *The Day We Got Drunk on Cake*, and his characteriza-tion depends, in the way of the modern free story, on the gradual accumulation of concrete but highly suggestive details that keep pointing to the gap between what Malcolmson is and what he perceives himself to be. The first sentence of the story, describing Malcolmson arriving at his former wife's house to pick up his two daughters for their weekly outing together, exemplifies the way that small details in this story are charged with suggestion: "Malcolmson, a fair, tallish man in a green tweed suit that required pressing, banged the driver's door of his ten-year-old Volvo and walked quickly away from the car, jangling the keys."[15] The information almost thrown away here – the suit needs pressing, the car is ten years old – points to the true nature of Malcolmson's deteriorating character, just as the abruptness and harshness of his actions, reinforced through the jarring assonantal "banged" and "jangling," suggest the lack of control, largely induced by alcohol, that has come to define his life.

The story also discloses the futility of Malcolmson's life, and of his hopes of remarrying his wife Elizabeth and restoring his life to what it once was, by playing Malcolmson's consciousness off against other, more objective points of view. For example, when Malcolmson takes his daughters to the park, the memory of another, earlier scene in the park surfaces, and it jolts the reader into seeing Malcolmson from a disturbingly different position than the largely sympathetic one that has been operating up to this point:

In the drizzle they played a game among the trees, hiding and chasing one another. Once when they'd been playing this game a woman had brought a policeman up to him. She'd seen him approaching the girls, she said; the girls had been playing alone and he'd joined in. 'He's our daddy,' Susie had said, but the woman had still argued, claiming that he'd given them sweets so that they'd say that. 'Look at him,' the woman had insultingly said. 'He needs a shave.' Then she'd gone away, and the policeman had apologized.

(p. 9)

The most dramatic use of this technique occurs at the climax of the story, in the conversation that Malcolmson has with Elizabeth when he returns the girls at the end of the day. The gap between Malcolmson's point of view, embodying his hopes of redeeming himself from his life of alienation and loneliness, and the reality of how far he has fallen from that possibility, steadily widens as the story progresses, and in this scene, the shift to the relative objectivity of dialogue and, at one point, to Elizabeth's consciousness, seriously discredits Malcolmson's position, but without destroying the reader's sympathy for him:

'Will you think about it?'

'About what?'

'About our being together again.'

'Oh, for heaven's sake.' She turned away from him. 'I wish you'd go now,' she said.

'Will you come out with me on our birthday?'

'I've told you.' Her voice was loud and angry, her cheeks flushed. 'Can't you understand? I'm going to marry Richard. We'll be married within a month, when the girls have had time to get to know him a little better. By Christmas we'll be married.'

He shook his head in a way that annoyed her, seeming in his drunkenness to deny the truth of what she was saying. He tried to light a cigarette; matches dropped to the floor at his feet. He left them there.

It enraged her that he was sitting in an armchair in her flat with his eyelids drooping through drink and an unlighted cigarette in his hand and his matches spilt all over the floor. They were his children, but she wasn't his wife: he'd destroyed her as a wife, he'd insulted her, he'd left her to bleed and she had called him a murderer.

'Our birthday,' he said, smiling at her as though already she had agreed to join him on that day. 'And Hitler's and the Queen's.'

'On our birthday if I go out with anyone it'll be Richard.'

'Our birthday is beyond the time –'

'For God's sake, there is no beyond the time. I'm in love with another man –'

'No.'

'On our birthday,' she shouted at him, 'on the night of our birthday Richard will make love to me in the bed you slept in for nine years. You have access to the children. You can demand no more.'

(pp. 24–5)

This scene does not lead to any epiphany of self-understanding for Malcolmson. Indeed, part of the pathos of Malcolmson's character is that his illusions are so powerfully, so desperately a part of his life that they cannot be dislodged, even by such an encounter. And so just as Raymond Bamber retreats after his disturbing confrontation with Mrs Fitch to the psychological safe-harbor of his misconceptions, so Malcolmson, at the end of "Access to the Children," is left clinging to the illusions without which he could not live. He leaves Elizabeth's flat, and stops off, as he always does on Sunday evenings, at a nearby pub:

'D'you understand me?' he drunkenly asked the barmaid. 'It's *too* ridiculous to be true – that man will go because none of it makes sense the way it is.' The barmaid smiled again and nodded. He bought her a glass of beer, which was something he did every Sunday night. He wept as he paid for it, and touched his cheeks with the tips of his fingers to wipe away the tears. Every Sunday he wept, at the end of the day, after he'd had his access. The barmaid raised her glass, as always she did. They drank to the day that was to come, when the error he had made would be wiped away, when the happy marriage could continue. 'Ridiculous,' he said. 'Of course it is.'

(p. 29)

"The Grass Widows" also concerns a failed marriage, but viewed primarily from the point of view of the wife. The marriage of Mrs Angusthorpe, the story's principal center of consciousness, is characterized by the ruthless psychological domination of an unloving husband and by Mrs Angusthorpe's resignation to a life of disappointment. In the course of the story, Mrs Angusthorpe is prodded out of her lethargic alienation, but ultimately with the same ineffectuality that marks the responses of many other of Trevor's characters when faced to force the truth about themselves.

The unjust balance of the Angusthorpes' marriage is threatened by two events that upset the English couple's regular summer holiday in Co. Galway: a dramatic decline in the quality of the hotel that they stay in, following the death of the old proprietor who is then replaced by his crass, greedy son; and the unexpected arrival at the hotel of a honeymooning couple, the husband turning out to be a former, and much favored, pupil of Mr Angusthorpe at the public school of which he is headmaster. The second of these two events is described in a scene marked by the kind of humor notably absent from the bleaker ''Access to the Children'':

> In the middle of the night, at midnight precisely, the Angusthorpes were awakened simultaneously by a noise from the room beyond the new partition.
>
> 'Put a pillow down, darling,' a male voice was saying as clearly as if its possessor stood in the room beside the Angusthorpes' bed.
>
> 'Couldn't we wait until another time?' a woman pleaded in reply. 'I don't see what good a pillow will do.'
>
> 'It'll lift you up a bit,' the man explained. 'It said in the book to put a pillow down if there was difficulty.'
>
> 'I don't see –'
>
> 'It'll make entry easier,' said the man. 'It's a well-known thing.'
>
> Mrs Angusthorpe switched on her bedside light and saw that her husband was pretending to be asleep. 'I'm going to rap on the wall,' she whispered. 'It's disgusting, listening to this.'
>
> 'I think I'm going down,' said the man.
>
> 'My God,' whispered Mr Angusthorpe, opening his eyes. 'It's Jackson Major.'
>
> (p. 185)

The action that Mrs Angusthorpe finally takes, when it becomes clear that her husband will not leave the hotel for her sake, is more pathetic than courageous, and by its nature precludes any possibility of self-understanding or a change in the quality of her marriage. Rather than confront her husband about the state of their marriage, she tries to convince Daphne Jackson to leave her husband, drawing parallels between the way that her husband treated her at the beginning of their marriage and the way that Daphne's husband has been treating her. Throughout this conversation, Mrs Angusthorpe's consciousness is central, and the narration superimposes on her warnings and urgings to Daphne another scene, projected in Mrs Angusthorpe's imagination, in which Mrs Angusthorpe is telling her husband that Jackson Major's wife has left him: "She would watch him sitting there in all his dignity: she would wait until he was about to pass a forkful of food to his mouth and then she would say: 'Jackson Major's wife has left him already.' And she would smile at him" (p. 198). The motive disclosed here is anything but selfless or compassionate; Mrs Angusthorpe has obviously been driven to the futile position of seeing her marriage principally as a power struggle, and is using the Jackson-Majors to gain some leverage over her husband.

Whatever her motives, there is truth at the center of Mrs Angusthorpe's warnings to Daphne. But like so many of Trevor's truth-tellers, Mrs Angusthorpe is ignored, and the story ends in multiple ironies: Mrs Angusthorpe retreats to a marriage from which, it is clearer now than ever, she will never be able to escape, and Daphne, clinging to the same kind of illusions that have permitted Mrs Angusthorpe to spend forty years in a bad marriage, seems trapped in an equally hopeless relationship. The story's final scene, in which the two couples are rearranged into male and female pairs, shows Mrs Angusthorpe, like Mr Jeffs at the end of "The Table," withdrawing into her world of timid resignation, and Daphne Jackson, like Raymond Bamber at the end of "Raymond Bamber and Mrs Fitch," into her world of wilful illusions:

> 'I'm sorry if I upset you,' Mrs Angusthorpe said to her, touching her arm to hold her back for a moment. 'I'm afraid my temper ran away with me.'
>
> The two men went ahead, involved in a new conversation. 'We might try that little tributary this afternoon,' the headmaster was suggesting.
>
> 'I sat there afterwards, seeing how horrid it must have been for you,' Mrs Angusthorpe said. 'I was only angry at the prospect of an unpleasant fortnight. I took it out on you.'
>
> 'Don't worry about it.'
>
> 'One should keep one's anger to oneself. I feel embarrassed now,' said Mrs Angusthorpe . . .
>
> 'I think we must go in now, Mrs Angusthorpe,' Daphne said.

In her weariness she smiled at Mrs Angusthorpe, suddenly sorry
for her because she had so wretched a marriage that it caused
her to become emotional with strangers.

(pp. 205–6)

Mrs Angusthorpe exemplifies a tendency in Trevor's fiction to
see women as victims of domineering, uncaring, or failed men –
from Mrs Jaraby in *The Old Boys* to Doris Smith and Julia Ferndale in *Other People's Worlds*.[16] However much responsibility they
may bear for their oppressed states, these women, as victims,
embody both the human costs of the collapse of love and the
broader principle of alienation and disconnection.

The psychologically and emotionally crippling effects of illusions
– a major concern of stories like "The Grass Widows" and
"Access to the Children" – are explored more extensively in the
title story of *Angels at the Ritz*, Trevor's next collection. Although
it employs a conventional enough plot, the events of a wife-
swapping party in suburban London, this story is one of Trevor's
most ambitious. It examines the moral consequences of construct-
ing not just individual lives but an entire community around
pretence and illusion, and at the same time dramatizes powerfully
the passage from the relative innocence of young adulthood to the
compromises and losses that define middle age.[17]

The story relies on a center of consciousness, Polly Dillard, who
is both part of and separate from the world that the story
describes. As the wife of a successful advertising man, a mother,
and an active member of her community, Polly exemplifies much
of contemporary suburban life. But, as becomes clear the night she
realizes that her best friend, Sue Ryder, is trying to seduce her
husband, Gavin, at a party, Polly also stands apart; at least she
sees herself as more objective than the rest of her friends and
family, less given to living with illusions:

He [Gavin] believed she hadn't fallen as he and the Ryders had,
that middle age had dealt no awful blows. In a way that seemed
true to Polly, for it had often occurred to her that she, more
than the other three, had survived the outer suburb. She was
aware of pretences but could not pretend herself. She knew
everytime they walked into the local Tonino's that the local
Tonino's was just an Italian joke, a sham compared with the
reality of the original in Greek Street. She knew the party

they'd just been to was a squalid little mess. She knew that when Gavin enthused about a fifteen-second commercial for soap his enthusiasm was no cause for celebration. She knew the suburb for what it was, its Volvos and Vauxhalls, its paved paths in unfenced front gardens, its crescents and avenues and immature trees, and the games its people played.[18]

What Polly comes to realize by the end of the story, after Gavin has taken her home and returned alone to the party, is a larger irony – that her perception of the truth about her life, her moral superiority, cannot prevent the "awful blows" of middle age, the inevitable compromises and corruptions that come with time. It may be true, as she says, that she has not fallen into the overt deception and hypocrisy, embodied in the wife-swapping party, that have come to govern the lives of her husband and their friends, but she also recognizes, in the final epiphany of the story, that nothing can protect her from falling into middle age, from the gradual dulling of her moral sensibility. Nothing, in other words, can protect her from time – time the destroyer, time the killer, as the narrator of "The Day We Got Drunk on Cake" would put it. "Angels at the Ritz" concludes:

> The outer suburb was what it was, so was the shell of middle age: she didn't complain because it would be silly to complain when you were fed and clothed and comfortable, when your children were cared for and warm, when you were loved and respected. You couldn't forever weep with anger, or loudly deplore yourself and other people. You couldn't hit out with your fists as though you were back at the Misses Summers' nursery school in Putney. You couldn't forever laugh among the waiters at the Ritz just because it was fun to be there.
>
> In bed she poured herself a cup of tea, telling herself that what had happened tonight – and what was probably happening now – was reasonable and even fair. She had rejected what was distasteful to her, he had stood by her and had respected her feelings; his unfaithfulness seemed his due. In her middle-age calmness that was how she felt. She couldn't help it.
>
> It was how she had fallen, she said to herself, but all that sounded silly now.

(pp. 66–7)

In his novels, Trevor frequently employs juxtapositions between past and present to deepen character. In "Angels at the Ritz," frequent juxtapositions of scenes from the early years of the Dillards' marriage with the events of the night of the wife-swapping party also advance the story's main thematic concerns, forecasting and embodying the realization about the morally deadening effects of time that Polly comes to at the end of the story. The most important instance of this is the flashback to Polly's twenty-second birthday, which she and Gavin celebrated with the Ryders by going to dinner, recklessly, at the Ritz:

> Sitting in the restaurant with people she liked, she'd thought it was the nicest thing that had ever happened to her on her birthday. It was absurd to go to the Ritz for a birthday treat: martinis in the Rivoli Bar because Malcolm said it was the thing, the gilt chairs and the ferns. But the absurdity hadn't mattered because in those days nothing much did. It was fun, they enjoyed being together, they had a lot to be happy about. Malcolm might yet play rugby for England. Gavin was about to make his breakthrough into films. Sue was pretty, and Polly that night felt beautiful. They had sat there carelessly laughing, while deferential waiters simulated the gaiety of their mood. They had drunk champagne because Malcolm said they must.
>
> With Malcolm still holding her hand, she crossed the spacious hall of Number Four Sandiway Crescent. People were beginning to leave. Malcolm released his hold of her in order to bid them goodbye.
>
> She stood in the doorway of the sitting-room watching Gavin and Sue dancing. She lifted her brandy glass to her lips and drank from it calmly. Her oldest friend was attempting to seduce her husband, and for the first time in her life she disliked her.

(pp. 59–60)

That devastating transition from drinking champagne at the Ritz "because Malcolm said they must" to Malcolm holding Polly's hand as they cross the hall of the Ryders' suburban house defines precisely and dramatically the distance between innocence and experience, between youth and middle age.

Another highly accomplished story in *Angels at the Ritz*, "Mrs Silly," looks at a broken marriage from the point of view of a child. The story is based on a relatively conventional initiation-story plot: its principal character, a young boy named Michael, is caught between childhood and adolescence, dependence and independence, his family and the world beyond. But Trevor escalates the moral stakes by portraying Michael also as a victim of the break between his parents, placed midway between his mother, who has raised him on her own since being divorced from his father, and his well-to-do father, remarried to a young, smart-looking woman named Gillian.

Much of the story's effectiveness depends on the way in which it dramatizes the ambivalence in Michael's mind. The plot turns on Michael's going away to boarding school, but the usual identity problems accompanying such a move are complicated and intensified by the association of the school with Michael's father, who once was a student there. Also, his experience at school forces him to notice the contrast between the relative poverty and poor taste of his mother and the wealth and good taste of his father and Gillian. On his mother's first visit to the school, all this is dramatized by means of a specific, concrete scene that, in the vein of Trevor's writing, employs a third-person narrative voice identified closely with Michael's perception:

> She was wearing a headscarf and a maroon coat and another scarf at her neck. Her handbag was maroon also, but it was old, with something broken on one of the buckles: it was the handbag, he said to himself, that made you think she was cheaply dressed.
>
> He left the door and went to her, taking her arm. He felt ashamed that he'd thought her clothes were cheap-looking. She'd been upset when he'd told her that the rug had been sent by Gillian. She'd been upset and he hadn't bothered.
>
> 'Oh, Mummy,' he said.
>
> She hugged him to her, and when he looked up into her face he saw the mark of a tear on one of her cheeks. Her fluffy hair was sticking out a bit beneath the headscarf, her round, plump face was forcing itself to smile.
>
> (p. 79)

The contrast here between Michael's action and exclamation and his coldly accurate observations of his mother's appearance defines precisely the psychological distance that he is forced to travel in the story. Moreover, those final, unavoidable perceptions of the dirtied cheek and unruly hair, made even at the moment of his most childish expression of affection, forecast the end of the story, and Michael's final, public rejection of his mother.

Perhaps because its center of consciousness is a child, "Mrs Silly" manages to achieve considerable psychological authenticity and complexity with very few incursions into the past. None the less, there are often very real advantages to be had from the kind of juxtapositions between past and present observed in "Angels at the Ritz." Some of these advantages can be seen by reading a story from *Angels at the Ritz* entitled "A Complicated Nature" against the earlier, and on the surface quite similar, "Raymond Bamber and Mrs Fitch."

The central character in each story – Attridge in "A Complicated Nature" and Raymond Bamber in "Raymond Bamber and Mrs Fitch" – is a repressed, shy, solipsistic bachelor who, in the course of the story, finds his introverted values threatened or challenged by an encounter with an aggressive woman, Mrs Fitch in the earlier story and Mrs Matera in the later one. Nothing could be more repellent, in fact, to the controlled fastidious life that Attridge has made for himself than the story that Mrs Matera, a neighbor, brings to his doorstep: that her lover has just died, apparently of a heart-attack, while making adulterous love to her in her flat.

In "Raymond Bamber and Mrs Fitch," the confrontation between the two different characters, taking place in the fictional present, is the entire story; in "A Complicated Nature," on the other hand, Mrs Matera's intrusion opens the door into Attridge's past, and her story is frequently juxtaposed with Attridge's memories of the one great failure of his life, a marriage destroyed by his emotional and sexual inadequacies. These juxtapositions not only develop Attridge's character in a way that Raymond Bamber's is never accounted for, but they also create an ironic tension that undermines Attridge's seemingly compassionate decision to do what he can, despite all his instincts, to help Mrs Matera. Just as Mrs Angusthorpe, in "The Grass Widows," tries to rescue Daphne Jackson because of her own desire for revenge against her husband, so Attridge acts less out of genuine compassion than out of a need to prove to himself that he is capable of compassion, and thereby to protect himself from the truth about his emotional paralysis. And so the juxtapositions of past and present reveal both the futility and self-deception of Attridge's character and the impossibility of any kind of redemption from his life of disconnection. The following scene, which moves from surface events to Attridge's apparent motives and finally to his undercutting memories, is characteristic:

'I wouldn't bother you,' she said, 'if I could manage on my own.' She would have telephoned a friend, she said, except there wouldn't be time for a friend to get to the block of flats. 'There's very little time, you see,' she said.

It was then, while she spoke those words, that Attridge felt the first hint of excitement. It was the same kind of excitement that he experienced just before the final curtain of *Tannhäuser*, or whenever, in the Uffizi, he looked upon Credi's Annunciation. Mrs Matera was a wretched, unattractive creature who had been conducting a typical hole-in-the-corner affair and had received her just rewards. It was hard to feel sorry for her, and yet for some reason it was harder not to. The man who had died had got off scot-free, leaving her to face the music miserably on her own. 'You're inhuman,' his ex-wife had said in Siena. 'You're incapable of love. Or sympathy, or anything else.' She'd stood there in her underclothes, taunting him.

(p. 124)

Given this, the story's final ironic twist – Mrs Matera's lover suddenly appears alive and well, the victim of a temporary blackout, not a heart-attack – which robs Attridge of the opportunity to act, seems perfectly appropriate, as is Attridge's final Bamber-like retreat into the illusions and self-deceptions that, as the irony in this passage makes clear, make possible his life of alienation:

He had always been a little on the cold side, he knew that well. But his ex-wife might have drawn on the other aspects of his nature and dispelled the coldness. Instead of displaying all that impatience, she might have cosseted him and accepted his complications. The love she sought would have come in its own good time, as sympathy and compassion had eventually come that afternoon. Warmth was buried deep in some people, he wanted to say to the two faces in the hall, but he knew that, like his ex-wife, the faces would not understand.

(p. 131)

Although this kind of exploration of a character's past occurs in a number of the stories in Trevor's first three collections, little interest is paid in them to the public past, to history; the focus is usually domestic and the time-frame almost without exception contemporary. With the publication of *Lovers of Their Time*, however, Trevor's stories begin increasingly to see human character as determined by social and political forces, including the forces of history. This is especially true for Trevor's stories about Ireland, but a number of non-Irish stories, including one of Trevor's finest pieces of fiction, the three-story sequence "Matilda's England," also reflect this developing concern.

The first story in the volume, "Broken Homes," bears a number of resemblances to earlier Trevor stories. For one thing, it turns on a confrontation between two radically different kinds of characters – an elderly, orderly, fastidious widow, Mrs Malby, and a group of unruly adolescents, who, as part of a social worker's plan to help them, are brought in to paint Mrs Malby's flat, and in the process terrorize her and all but destroy her home. Mrs Malby is a familiar figure in Trevor's fiction, and Trevor's capacity for characterizing the fears and strengths of the elderly – observable in his work from *The Old Boys* on – is well represented in this story. The adolescents, and especially their inability to make moral judgments, are also familiar; Timothy Gedge in *The Children of Dynmouth* and Joy Smith in *Other People's Worlds* come immediately to mind. In the following scene, the moral casualness and indifference of the young people and the unbridgeable distance between them and the generation represented by Mrs Malby are dramatized chiefly through dialogue:

She left the bathroom; the blare of the transistor still persisted. She didn't want to sit in her sitting-room, having to listen to it. She climbed the stairs to her bedroom, imagining the coolness there, and the quietness.

'Hey,' the girl protested when Mrs Malby opened her bedroom door.

'Sod off, you guys,' the boy with the red hair ordered. They were in her bed. Their clothes were all over the floor.

Her two budgerigars were flying about the room. Protruding

from sheets and blankets she could see the boy's naked shoulders and the back of his head. The girl poked her face up from under him. She gazed at Mrs Malby. 'It's not them,' she whispered to the boy. 'It's the woman.'

'Hi there, missus.' The boy twisted his head round. From the kitchen, still loudly, came the noise of the transistor.

'Sorry,' the girl said.

'Why are they up here? Why have you let my birds out? You've no right to behave like this.'

'We needed sex,' the girl explained.

The budgerigars were perched on the looking-glass on the dressing-table, beadily surveying the scene.

'They're really great, them budgies,' the boy said.[19]

But what distinguishes "Broken Homes" from many earlier Trevor stories is its assertion that the lives of Mrs Malby and the adolescents have been shaped by history. The title of the story refers to more than the domestic environments of the teenagers or to what the teenagers do to Mrs Malby's peaceful life; Mrs Malby's home was, in fact, broken long before these young people, symbols and symptoms of the collapse of moral values in contemporary society, arrived on her doorstep. Both Mrs Malby's sons have been killed in the Second World War, and by juxtaposing Mrs Malby's memories of their deaths with her helpless witnessing of the adolescents' destruction of her flat, the story suggests a strong, causal connection between the specific past of the war and the specific present represented by the adolescents. The most significant of these scenes occurs at the end of the story, after a teacher from the young persons' school has been summoned to calm Mrs Malby:

She thought of her two sons, Eric and Roy, not knowing quite why she thought of them now. She descended the stairs with the teacher, who was cheerfully talking about community relations. You had to make allowances, he said, for kids like that; you had to try and understand; you couldn't just walk away.

Quite suddenly she wanted to tell him about Eric and Roy. In the desire to talk about them she imagined their bodies, as she used to in the past, soon after they'd been killed. They lay on the desert sand, desert birds swooped down on them. Their four eyes were gone. She wanted to explain to the teacher that

109

they'd been happy, a contented family in Agnes Street, until the
war came and smashed everything to pieces.

(pp. 25–6)

This implicit argument that the contemporary, alienated world
is, in important ways, the product of the personal and social
destruction wreaked by a world war is made explicit and
considerably extended in "Matilda's England." The view that
history cannot be escaped, and that the private and the public are
inextricably bound together, is insisted on again and again in this
sequence of three stories – in the structure of each of them, in the
way that they depend on and play off each other, in the
developments of their related plots, and in the central character of
all three, Matilda.[20] The governing paradigm of a loss of
innocence, of a fall into a world of experience that threatens to
destroy protective illusions, in these stories describes not just
individual characters but modern civilization as a whole, and the
madness that overwhelms the protagonist in the final story is also
the madness of a society warped and dismembered by the stagger-
ing, fragmenting force of two world wars.

In the first story, "The Tennis Court," the primary victim of
this devastation is the elderly Mrs Ashburton, the only survivor of
a once-powerful family that owned and ran Challacombe Manor,
a large country estate, before Mrs Ashburton's husband was
severely shell-shocked in the First World War. But the story is told
in the first-person from the point of view of Matilda, who is 9
years old at the time and the daughter of one of the families that
now farm the land; and it is essentially Matilda's story, since what
matters most is the impression that events make on her
consciousness, and since she will, by the end of the sequence, have
replaced Mrs Ashburton as history's victim.

The plot of "The Tennis Court" concerns Mrs Ashburton's
long-harbored plans to restore the tennis court at Challacombe
Manor, and to throw a grand tennis party of the order of those
once held regularly in the days before the war. And although she
gets her wish, with the help of Matilda's older brother Dick and
older sister Betty, the story ends on a note of resounding irony,
a moment that Matilda will not understand until later in her life.
The day of the party falls on 31 August 1939, and when it is over,
Matilda and a friend find Mrs Ashburton sitting alone in her

110

darkened kitchen:

> It was darker in the kitchen than it was outside, almost pitch-dark because the windows were so dirty that even in daytime it was gloomy.
>
> 'Matilda,' Mrs Ashburton said. She was sitting in an arm-chair by the oil-stove. I knew she was because that was where her voice came from. We couldn't see her.
>
> 'We came to say goodbye, Mrs Ashburton.'
>
> She told us to wait. She had a saucer of chocolate for us, she said, and we heard her rooting about on the table beside her. We heard the glass being removed from a lamp and then she struck a match. She lit the wick and put the glass back. In the glow of lamplight she looked exhausted. Her eyes seemed to have receded, the thinness of her face was almost sinister.
>
> We ate our chocolate in the kitchen that smelt of oil, and Mrs Ashburton didn't speak. We said goodbye again, but she didn't say anything. She didn't even nod or shake her head. She didn't kiss me like she usually did, so I went and kissed her instead. The skin of her face felt like crinkled papers.
>
> 'I've had a very happy day,' she said when Belle Frye and I had reached the kitchen door. 'I've had a lovely day,' she said, not seeming to be talking to us but to herself. She was crying, and she smiled in the lamplight, looking straight ahead of her. 'It's all over,' she said. 'Yet again.'

(pp. 59–60)

In this scene, Trevor exploits fully the advantages of the limited point of view that he so rarely uses. Only an unconscious awareness of the truth, felt in the vaguely dark associations that register on Matilda's young sensibility – the lack of light, the ''almost sinister'' look of Mrs Ashburton's defeated expression, the decayed feel of her skin – is allowed to penetrate the veil of childish innocence that surrounds Matilda at this point. But this moment of supreme irony – the Second World War beginning on the very day on which all of Mrs Ashburton's efforts to recreate the Edenic life of pre First World War civilization culminate – does, however dimly perceived, shape Matilda's consciousness, setting up precisely the conditions for her own fall into experience during the Second World War, and providing a model victim, obsessed with a past that cannot be recovered, whom Matilda will live to emulate.

The entire three-story sequence is constructed around parallels and echoes that reinforce the idea of the relentless, increasingly destructive momentum of history. In the second story, for example, "The Summer-House," the loss of Mrs Ashburton's husband's sanity in the First World War is recast and intensified in the deaths of Matilda's father and brother in the Second World War. Also, the general paradigm of a loss of innocence is advanced through changes in Matilda's character. Her consciousness is more knowing in this story, which is set three years after the end of "The Tennis Court," and her own fall into experience is embodied in the discovery, after her father's death, that her mother has a lover, a man whom she has been meeting clandestinely in the summerhouse at Challacombe Manor.

The scene in which her mother tells Matilda and Betty that she is going to marry this man insists on the connections between the large-scale destruction of innocence embodied in the war and the explosion of Matilda's once seemingly secure childhood and family life. This scene also, in its nervous, staccato syntax and its attention to certain imagined details, hints at an unbalanced quality to Matilda's mind, looking back to Mrs Ashburton's husband, if not to Mrs Ashburton herself, and ahead to the madness that will overtake Matilda in the third story of the sequence:

> 'He could never come here now,' Betty said to my mother. 'You couldn't do it to Matilda.'
> I didn't know why she should have particularly mentioned me since it concerned us all, and anyway I felt it was too late to bother about me. Too much had happened. I felt I'd been blown to pieces, as if I'd been in the war myself, as if I'd been defeated by it, as old Mrs Ashburton had been defeated by her war. The man would come to live in the farmhouse. He would wear my father's clothes. He would sit by the range, reading the newspaper. He would eat at the table, and smile at me with his narrow teeth.

> (p. 87)

Cruelty, Mrs Ashburton used to tell Matilda, is natural in wartime, something one has to get used to. Only now, having been struck by the same hand of history that shattered Mrs Ashburton's life, and having lost many of her illusions in the process, including her faith in a benevolent God ("Praying seemed nonsense. . . . He [God] wasn't there to listen to what you prayed for. God was something else, something harder and more awful and more frightening'' (p. 88)), can Matilda begin to understand fully the significance of what Mrs Ashburton told her. "At the time I hadn't understood what she'd meant,'' she thinks at the story's conclusion, "but I could feel the cruelty she'd spoken of now. I could feel it in myself'' (p. 88).

In the third story, "The Drawing-Room,'' Matilda is in her twenties, and this cruelty has driven her mad. Her illness takes the form of a pathological identification with Mrs Ashburton and an illusionary belief that she can erase the devastation caused by two world wars by recreating at Challacombe Manor the world as it was before the wars, the world that Mrs Ashburton tried to create, if only for a moment, in her tennis party on that unlucky August day in 1939. Her means of doing this – her doomed, sacrificial marriage to Ralph Gregory, the son of a vulgar middle-class couple who buy Challacombe Manor with profits made from the war – constitute an act of wilful blindness to reality, a fierce deter- mination to reject the contemporary world that has survived the wars. She says of the day of their marriage:

> I was there in my wedding-dress, married to Ralphie, who wasn't unkind; Challacombe Manor was as it used to be in its heydey, it was as Mrs Ashburton had known it as a bride also. Going to live there and watching over it seemed to make up for everything, for all the bad things that had happened, my father's death, and Dick's.
>
> (p. 106)

In keeping with the pattern of escalating stakes in the sequence, this illusion is considerably more deranged and dangerous than are Mrs Ashburton's plans for throwing one last tennis party in the old style; Matilda is sacrificing her life to an obsession with a largely imaginary Edenic past, and the result is that her uncon- summated marriage, like similar relationships in much of Trevor's fiction, becomes just one more condition of her alienation.

As all this suggests, much of the effect of this story is cumulative, resting on resonances between it and the two earlier stories in the sequence. But the story also depends considerably on the dramatization of Matilda's madness. This, in turn, is partly a product of Trevor's use of first-person narrative, the way in which

113

Matilda's condition has to be discerned by the reader through the smoke-screen of her rationalizations and self-justifications. It also depends on the way in which evidence of Matilda's growing madness is released gradually in the course of the story, moving from an apparently benign obsession with the past to the revelation of serious gaps in her memory, to casually mentioned experiences of seeing Mrs Ashburton in the house, and finally to the party at Challacombe Manor at which Matilda's madness erupts fully. This last scene is careful to maintain sympathy for Matilda, presenting her as victim as well as victimizer:

> I was alone in the dining-room, as I'd guessed I would be. But it wasn't any longer a room you could be quiet in. Everything seemed garish, the red glitter of the wine bottles, the red candles, dish after dish of different food, the cheeses. It made me angry that Mrs Gregary and Mrs Absom should have come to Challacombe Manor in order to instruct Mrs Stritch, that Mrs Gregary should strut about in the drawing-room, telling people who she was.
>
> I jumbled the food about, dropping pieces of meat into the bowls of cream, covering the tarts with salad. I emptied two wine bottles over everything, watching the red stain spreading on the table-cloth and on the cheeses. They had no right to be in the house, their Daimler had no right to be in the garage.
>
> (p. 116)

Although the main events of "The Drawing-Room" take place in the early 1950s, when Matilda is a young woman, the story is told inside a framework in which Matilda, at the age of 48, is writing the story while sitting in the drawing-room of Challacombe Manor. She is old before her time ("I feel like a woman of sixty," she says (p. 89)), alone with her obsessions, the quintessential alienated victim. And although she says she feels sorry for the way that she treated Ralph, that she was unaccountably possessed by the cruelty that Mrs Ashburton used to tell her about, there is no possibility of redemption; Ralph will never come back, as she knows, and she is left in a world that she can no longer recognize:

> I sit here now in her drawing-room, and may perhaps become as old as she was. Sometimes I walk up to the meadow where

the path to school was, but the meadow isn't there any more.
There are rows of coloured caravans and motor-cars and shacks.
In the garden I can hear the voices of people drifting down to
me, and the sound of music from their wireless sets. Nothing is
like it was.

(p. 125)

Her madness is, for Trevor, a means of registering the effect of the
whole curve of modern history, from the pre-war days when
Challacombe Manor was thriving economically and culturally to
the ragged, shiftless world of our contemporary age.

The title story of *Lovers of Their Time* is less conscious of history
than is "Matilda's England," but it does insist on seeing human
character as significantly shaped by social or cultural forces. As its
title suggests, "Lovers of Their Time" concerns a love-affair that
is conditional, a product of a certain age, the 1960s; everything in
the story suggests that the relationship between Norman Britt, a
travel agent, and Marie, a young girl working as a clerk in a
chemist's shop, could not have occurred in any other, less reckless
decade. Trevor gives the affair its romantic due, its moments of
genuinely felt passion and lyricism. But the same relentless irony
that informs almost all his short stories is at work as well, qualifying the affair, suggesting the presence of forces that will inevitably
destroy this precarious moment of human connection.

The ultimate futility of the relationship is insisted on largely
through the accumulation of many ironies. There is, for example,
Norman's job: he is a travel agent who never goes anywhere, a
man who makes arrangements to fulfill other people's dreams.
And there is his wife, the sour, sexually starved Hilda, whose
vulgarity and earthiness provide a strong counter-weight to the
romantic afflatus that Norman experiences with the innocent
Marie; it is Hilda that Norman must return to every night, after
his furtive meetings with Marie, and Hilda and her world are
portrayed in the most anti-romantic of terms, as in this passage:

Hilda was watching *Z-Cars* in the sitting-room, drinking V. P.
wine. His stuff was in the oven, she told him. . . .
'All right then?' she said as he carried his tray of food into
the sitting-room and sat down in front of the television set.
'Want some V. P., eh?'
Her eyes continued to watch the figures on the screen as she

spoke. He knew she'd prefer to be in the Folwers' house or at the Club, although now that they'd aquired a TV set the evenings passed easier when they were alone together.

'No thanks,' he said in reply to her offer of wine and he began to eat something that appeared to be a rissole. There were two of them, round and brown in a tin-foil container that also contained gravy. He hoped she wasn't going to be demanding in their bedroom. He eyed her, for sometimes he could tell.

'Hi,' she said, noticing the glance. 'Feeling fruity, dear?' She laughed and winked, her suggestive voice seeming odd as it issued from her thin, rather dried-up face.

(pp. 220–1)

There is also the irony of the setting in which Norman and Marie consummate their relationship, the bathroom of the Great Western Royal Hotel. Even the music of the 1960s, perhaps the most reliable barometer of the romantic spirit of that decade, is turned against Norman and Marie. In a bar, the couple overhear Elvis Presley's voice singing, "Take my hand, take my whole life too," a line that is, considering the potential consequences of Norman's trying to marry Marie, full of irony. And when the story marks the passage of time by shifting from Elvis to the Beatles, the specific allusion – "I believe in yesterday" – mocks an affair that in several years has not got beyond the fugitive, impermanent character that defined it at the beginning.

In the end, time – that final ironic deflator so present in earlier stories like "The Day We Got Drunk on Cake" and "Angels at the Ritz" – joins forces with everything working against Norman and Marie, and the affair, like the decade that inspired it, becomes part of the past. At the conclusion of the story, back in his humdrum life as travel agent and Hilda's reluctant husband, Norman has only his memories. Like the illusions that so many of Trevor's characters depend on to survive, these provide genuine psychological comfort. But, characteristically, Trevor spices this sympathetic view of Norman with a subtle, undermining irony suggesting that these romantic recollections, like illusions in general, are only masks to cover the alienation and loneliness that in fact define his life:

For Norman Britt, as the decade of the 1960s passed, it trailed behind it the marvels of his love affair with Marie. Hilda's scorn when he had confessed had not devalued them, nor had the two dirty rooms in Kilburn, nor the equally unpleasant experience in Reading. Their walk to the Great Western Royal, the drinks they could not afford in the hotel bar, their studied nonchalance as they made their way separately upstairs, seemed to Norman to be a fantasy that had miraculously become real. The second-floor bathroom belonged in it perfectly, the bathroom full of whispers and caressing, where the faraway places of his daily work acquired a hint of magic when he spoke of them to a girl as voluptuous as any of James Bond's. Sometimes on the Tube he would close his eyes and with the greatest pleasure that remained to him he would recall the delicately veined marble and the great brass taps, and the bath that was big enough for two. And now and again he heard what appeared to be the strum of distant music, and the voices of the Beatles celebrating a bathroom love, as they had celebrated Eleanor Rigby and other people of that time.

(p. 240)

The reference to the Beatles' "Eleanor Rigby" packs the story's final irony, insisting that Norman, despite his part in the decade of romance, is at heart, like Eleanor Rigby, just another of "all the lonely people."

The best of the stories in Trevor's two most recent collections, *Beyond the Pale* and *The News from Ireland*, are those in which the relationship between history and the individual is worked out against the backdrop of Ireland. None the less, although many of the non-Irish stories in these two books return to the relatively non-political concerns of Trevor's earlier stories, there are some notable exceptions, one of the most unusual of which is "The Blue Dress," from *Beyond the Pale*.

Although this account of a broken love-affair between a middle-aged journalist and the young daughter of a well-to-do country family employs Trevor's familiar objective correlative of failed love, the action takes place against a sharply etched political and social background, and the story insists on connections between private and public life. As a journalist, the story's central character, Terris, has developed the conviction that the world of public events is governed largely by hypocrisy and the covering up of moral wrongs, and this suspicion of appearances carries over

117

into his private life, eventually undermining his love-affair with Dorothea Lysarth. A story that Dorothea tells Terris about the death of a childhood companion who supposedly fell from a tree in the Lysarths' yard when they were playing together triggers another version of the event in Terris's imagination, in which Dorothea, out of spite and jealousy, pushes her companion out of the tree. In Terris's mind, the Lysarth family has conspired to cover up this event ever since.

Like Matilda in "Matilda's England," and like many other of Trevor's characters obsessed with what they see as the truth, Terris is considered mad; indeed, he is described as writing this first-person account from inside a mental institution, a situation that virtually guarantees that his version of what happened, like the versions of reality presented by Mrs Eckdorf and Miss Gomez, will not be taken seriously. The story's opening employs a highly impressionistic style – one that is, in fact, as close as Trevor gets to literary impressionism and stream-of-consciousness writing – to dramatize Terris's obsession with hypocrisy and corruption, and to do so with considerable psychological authenticity:

> My cinder-grey room has a window, but I have never in all my time here looked out of it. It's easier to remember, to conjure up this scene or that, to eavesdrop. Americans give arms away, Russians promise tanks. In Brussels an English politician break-fasts with his mistress; a pornographer pretends he's selling Christmas cards. Carefully I listen, as in childhood I listened to the hushed conversation of my parents.
>
> I stand in the cathedral at Vézelay, whose bishops once claimed it possessed the mortal remains of Mary Magdalene, a falseness which was exposed by Pope Boniface VIII. I wonder about that Pope, and then the scene is different.
>
> I sit in the Piazza San Marco on the day when I discovered a sea of corruption among the local Communists. The music plays, visitors remark upon the pigeons.
>
> Scenes coalesce: Miss MacNamara passes along the prom-enade, Major Trubstall lies, the blue dress flutters and is still. In Rotterdam I have a nameless woman. '*Feest wezen vieren?*' she says. '*Gedronken?*' In Corniglia the wine is purple, the path by the coast is marked as a lover's lane. I am silly, Dorothea says, the dress is just a dress. She laughs, like water running over pebbles.

I must try, they tell me; it will help to write it down. I do not argue, I do precisely as they say. Carefully, I remember. Carefully, I write it down.

(p. 110)

"Lunch in Winter," from *The News from Ireland*, also relies on a relatively impressionistic style, although written in the third person. In this story, which in terms of subject-matter is closer to Trevor's earlier work than to stories like "Matilda's England" or "Lovers of Their Time," Trevor abandons his characteristic modulation of narrative voice between objectivity and subjectivity in favor of a voice that is dominated if not overwhelmed by the story's protagonist, a former chorus girl named Nancy Simpson. On the one hand, as the opening paragraph of the story demonstrates, that voice can be made a vehicle for the naive romanticism, the pathetic clinging to illusions and the past that define part of Nancy's character:

Mrs Nancy Simpson – who did not at all care for that name and would have wished to be Nancy le Puys or Nancy du Maurier – awoke on a December morning. She had been dreaming of a time long past in her life, when her name had been Nancy Dawes, before she'd been married to anyone. The band had been playing *You are my Honeysuckle* and in the wings of the Old Gaiety they had all been in line, smiles ready, waiting to come on. *You are my honey-suckle, I am the bee* . . . Was it called something else, known by some other title? *Smoke Gets in your Eyes* had once been called something else, so Laurie Henderson had said, although, God knows, if Laurie'd said it it probably wasn't true. You could never tell with songs. *If You were the Only Girl in the World*, for instance: was that the full title or was it *If You were the Only Girl in the World and I was the Only Boy*? She'd had an argument with Laurie about that, a ridiculous all-night argument in Mrs Tomer's digs, Macclesfield, 1949 or '50. '50 probably because soon afterwards Laurie went down to London, doing something – barman probably – for the Festival of Britain thing. He'd walked out of Mrs Tomer's and she hadn't seen him for nine years. '51 actually it must have been. Definitely the Festival had been 1951.[21]

The narrative voice can also project another side of Nancy's personality – the casual indifference, the rejection of love and connection that embody Trevor's vision of alienation. Her thoughts about her children, for example, are recalled in the same morally evasive and immature language that marks the conversations of the adolescents in "Broken Homes":

Eventually she had gone to Canada with a man called Eddie Lush, whom later she had married. She had stayed there, and later in Philadelphia, for thirteen years, but when she returned to England two children who had been born, a boy and a girl, did not accompany her. They'd become more attached to Eddie Lush than to her, which had hurt her at the time, and there'd been accusations of neglect during the court case, which had been hurtful too. Once upon a time they'd written letters to her occasionally, but she wasn't sure now what they were doing.

(pp. 72–3)

Like many of Trevor's stories, "Lunch in Winter" ends with a retreat into protective but crippling illusions. The story's plot turns around a lunch that Nancy has with her first husband; even as he is proposing remarriage to her, she cannot stop flirting with their young Italian waiter, and in the end, her former husband dismisses her. Reflecting on this, Nancy is forced, for a moment, to face up to the true nature of her character; but by that evening, the experience has already been resigned to psychological oblivion, and she is able to look, with the pathetically false hope that her character embodies, toward a future that can never be realized:

'I think of you only,' she murmured in her soft whisper, feeling much better now because of the vodka and tonic, 'only wishing, wishing you were by my side.' When she'd come in at half-past five she'd noticed a chap booking in at the reception, some kind of foreign commercial traveller since the tennis people naturally didn't come in winter; fiftyish, handsomeish, not badly dressed. She was glad they hadn't turned on the television yet. From the corner where she sat she could see the stairs, where sooner or later the chap would appear. He'd buy a drink and then he'd look around and there she'd be.

(p. 84)

It may well be that the short story has flourished so remarkably in the twentieth century because it is peculiarly attuned to alienation and loneliness. It is, after all, an art form that tends to rely on fragments, innuendo, ambiguity – all of them properties of doubt or scepticism, of a philosophical view that sees everything as conditional.[22] Trevor's stories are very much in this tradition, both in terms of their narrative structures and strategies – their use of juxtaposition and parallelism, of suggestion and irony – and of the relatively bleak vision that seems to inform them. Frank O'Connor once said that the short story, at its most characteristic, has in it "something not often found in the novel – an intense awareness of human loneliness."[23] Certainly the characters in Trevor's stories – from Mr Jeffs to Nancy Simpson, from Malcolmson to Polly Dillard – are well-acquainted with that aspect of human nature, moving as they do through alienated and alienating worlds, and trailing behind them, as one character in a late story puts it, "such tales of woe."[24]

6

"THE WEIGHT OF CIRCUMSTANCES":
The Irish Fiction

There are passages in Trevor's writing about Ireland that place him squarely in the rich tradition, going back to Maria Edgeworth at the beginning of the nineteenth century, of Anglo-Irish Protestant fiction. This description, for example, of the ruins of a once elegant country house is, in its diction, rhythms, and elegaic tone, reminiscent of the work of twentieth-century Anglo-Irish novelists like Elizabeth Bowen or Molly Keane:

> When I reached its greatest height the burnt-out house lay below me, its stark outline beautiful against the pale landscape. Slowly I descended, clambering over a stone wall and through a gate, into the jungle of rhododendrons. The house, no longer beautiful, loomed grimly above me and around me, black walls exuding such damp bleakness that involuntarily I shivered. The weeds in the hall were less green, less vigorous than they had been that summer, and snow fell in the drawing-room you'd told me had once been scarlet. Lightly it lay on the mantelpiece and on the wreck of the grand piano; lengths of rough timber were nailed across an archway. I found the kitchen, and above it rooms that were undamaged. Nothing was locked, but there was no warmth in any of the rooms, and moisture seeped up the walls.[1]

The distinctly Anglo-Irish echoes of this passage – taken from Trevor's novel, *Fools of Fortune* (1983) – might be compared with another description from Trevor's work of a rural Irish landscape, this one, in its laconic rhythms, syntactical passivity, and ironic diction, as reminiscent of the Joyce of *Dubliners* as the first is of Bowen or Keane:

The dance-hall, owned by Mr Justin Dwyer, was miles from anywhere, a lone building by the roadside with treeless boglands all around and a gravel expanse in front of it. On pink pebbled cement its title was painted in an azure blue that matched the depth of the background shade yet stood out well, unfussily proclaiming *The Ballroom of Romance*. Above these letters four coloured bulbs – in red, green, orange and mauve – were lit at appropriate times, an indication that the evening rendezvous was open for business. Only the façade of the building was pink, the walls being a more ordinary grey. And inside, except for pink swing-doors, everything was blue.[2]

Both passages are characteristic of Trevor's Irish fiction. Indeed, it might be argued that no other contemporary writer concerned with Ireland has been better able to embrace both the country's Anglo-Irish Protestant heritage and its native Catholic tradition.[3] To some extent, this might be accounted for by the conditions of Trevor's life, especially the years of his childhood and adolescence spent shuttling back and forth between Protestant and Catholic social and school circles. But in more strictly literary terms, the capacity to accommodate two such different traditions implies an ability to see both from a certain distance. Trevor has himself suggested this in talking about the similarities between his early writing about England, when he was relatively new to that country, and his later writing about Ireland, when he had become something of a stranger to it:

I've always thought that writing books about this country [England] and especially a book like *The Old Boys*, which is a very English kind of book, is being like a photographer looking at a world from the outside. To me, England was an amazing and strange place. I'd never been outside of Ireland until I was twenty-two. When I *now* write about Ireland I'm doing a faintly similar thing, because I'm going back to a country which has become strange to me. Personally, I think that kind of thing is essential.[4]

The significance of Trevor's Irish writing has less to do, however, with its ability to speak with authenticity about the Ireland of Yeats and the Ireland of Joyce than with its capacity to draw on both those traditions in a way that ultimately transcends them. Written from the ironic distance that Trevor enjoys as an Anglo-Irishman writing about Catholic Ireland and, more generally, as a literary exile writing about his native country,[5] Trevor's Irish fiction needs to be read in terms of the broad moral concerns that govern his work as a whole, specifically the tension between a humanistic faith in compassion and connection and an ironic, qualifying assessment of contemporary life as alienated and disconnected. In the short story, "The Ballroom of Romance," the protagonist's father at one point reflects on the emotionally and psychologically crippled life of his daughter, describing himself as "saddened because the weight of circumstances had so harshly interfered with her life" (pp. 51–2). All of Trevor's work is concerned with "the weight of circumstances," with those alienating forces that constitute the ironic backdrop against which Trevor's characters seek, usually with limited success, freedom and fulfillment; in Trevor's fiction concerned with Ireland, those forces are particularly acute, that weight of circumstances particularly heavy.[6]

Trevor's writing about Ireland falls into two categories. On the one hand, there are a number of short stories and Trevor's one novella, *Nights at the Alexandra* (1987), that focus on the life of middle-class, provincial Ireland, depicting it as paralyzed and paralyzing.[7] Although these stories, in setting and character, owe something to the work of Frank O'Connor, they are rarely tempered by the bemused, forgiving sense of irony often found in O'Connor's stories; their vision tends to be bleak, and their master in this regard is clearly the Joyce of *Dubliners*. A second category of Trevor's Irish writing – consisting of *Fools of Fortune*, *The Silence in the Garden* (1988), and several short stories – is less strictly sociological in its portrayal of Ireland, and more conscious of political and historical forces as circumstances that limit individual freedom and fulfillment.[8] Like some of Trevor's non-Irish stories – "Matilda's England" and "Lovers of Their Time," for example – the Irish fiction of this type insists on seeing the past and the world of public events as constantly threatening to impinge on the private world of the individual. At the same time much of this work – especially that dealing with, directly or indirectly, the sectarian violence in contemporary Northern Ireland – affirms the moral responsibility of the individual to engage the world that lies beyond that of his private self.

The Joycean overtones of Trevor's earliest Irish stories, most of which are not concerned with history, are easy to find, particularly in the stories about childhood and adolesence. "An Evening with John Joe Dempsey" (*The Ballroom of Romance*), for example, might be compared to Joyce's "The Sisters," "An Encounter," or "Araby"; in all these stories, a young protagonist is led to a realization that the world of adult reality is corrupt and incomplete. Moreover, in Trevor's story, the man who serves as John Joe Dempsey's guide into this understanding is a rather Joycean figure – a middle-aged, alcoholic bachelor whose life has been sacrificed to an intensely religious and domineering mother. But Trevor's mark on this story is distinct. For one thing, although there is only one center of consciousness in the story – that of the protagonist – John Joe's fall from innocence depends on the juxtaposition of two radically different perspectives on the adult world; at the same time that John Joe is taking in the false and paralyzing piety preached at him in the pub by Mr Lynch, he is thinking about a retarded dwarf named Quigley, a Trevor-esque character who has been pouring into John Joe's innocent ears dark stories about the covert sex lives of the townspeople. The story ends in the kind of perfectly controlled balance between aspiration and desperation that characterizes much of Trevor's writing. As he gets into bed that night, John Joe tries to retreat into his private world of fantasy, where he is unencumbered by the adult realities – both hollowly pious and secretly prurient – that he has been exposed to:

> He entered his iron bed and the face of Mr Lynch passed from his mind and the voices of boys telling stories about freshly married couples faded away also. No one said to him now that he must not keep company with a crazed dwarf. In his iron bed, staring into the darkness, he made of the town what he wished to make of it, knowing that he would not be drawn away from his dreams by the tormenting fingers of a Christian Brother. In his iron bed, he heard again only the voice of the town's idiot and then that voice, too, was there no more. He travelled alone, visiting in his way the women of the town, adored and adoring, more alive in his bed than ever he was at the Christian Brothers' School, or in the grey Coliseum, or in the chip-shop, or Keogh's public house, or his mother's kitchen, more alive

than ever he would be at the sawmills. In his bed he entered a
paradise: it was grand being alone.

(pp. 153–4)

The irony here clearly owes something to Joyce – consider the
incomplete epiphanies at the end of "An Encounter" and
"Araby," for example – but what marks the passage as Trevor's
is the way in which it treads a fine line between sympathy and
irony, between a genuine celebration of John Joe's impulse to
transcend the confining, debilitating world of reality by remaking
it in his imagination – essentially the impulse of the artist – and
a recognition that such an aspiration is futile, that his life will
continue to be weighted down by the inescapable circumstances of
his religion, society, and family.

"The Ballroom of Romance," one of the most accomplished of
Trevor's early stories about rural Ireland, is also Joycean in its
outlines. The protagonist, a middle-aged spinster named Bridie
who has devoted her life to taking care of an elderly, crippled
father in their house in the remote hills, is a model of Joycean
paralysis. Moreover, the story turns on the destruction of Bridie's
illusions about her past – specifically, her highly romanticized
memories of a man named Patrick Grady, with whom she occasionally spent time at the shabby roadside dance-hall that gives the
story its ironic title – and therefore her possibilities for the future.
It is as dark a story as any of Joyce's accounts of similar
characters in "Eveline," "The Boarding House," "Clay," or "A
Mother." But the irony that generates this story's vision of futility
and alienation depends, characteristically for Trevor, at least as
much on the manipulation of narrative voice as on character and
situation. Because Bridie is the principal center of consciousness,
the story's third-person narrative voice is closely identified with
her, but at the same time it also contains, in ironic innuendos and
suggestions that run side by side with Bridie's point of view, the
seeds of its own undermining. The result is that perfectly
modulated balance between sympathy and irony observed in the
ending of "An Evening with John Joe Dempsey." In the following
passage, for example, Bridie's memories about Patrick Grady are
constantly subverted by an ironic note embedded in the narrative
voice:

It had been different, dancing with Patrick Grady, and she'd felt that he found it different dancing with her, although he'd never said so. At night she'd dreamed of him and in the daytime too, while she helped her mother in the kitchen or her father with the cows. Week by week she'd returned to the ballroom, smiling on its pink façade and dancing then in the arms of Patrick Grady. Often they'd stood together drinking lemonade, not saying anything, not knowing what to say. She knew he loved her, and she believed then that he would lead her one day from the dim, romantic ballroom, from its blueness and its pinkness and its crystal bowl of light and its music. She believed he would lead her into sunshine, to the town and the Church of Our Lady Queen of Heaven, to marriage and smiling faces. But someone else had got Patrick Grady, a girl from the town who'd never danced in the wayside ballroom. She'd scooped up Patrick Grady when he didn't have a chance.

(p. 60)

Much of the irony here is produced by a tension between an intimate, more or less sympathetic presentation of Bridie's feelings and a coldly realistic attitude that questions the validity and efficacy of those feelings. This runs throughout the passage, from the narrator's distancing qualifiers in the first sentence (''she'd felt that'' and ''although he'd never said so''), to the juxtapositions between Bridie's dreams of Patrick and her work in the kitchen and with the cows, and, at the end of the passage, to the shift from Bridie's litany-like reflections (''She knew he loved her'' and ''She believed he would lead her'') to the vulgar diction slipped into the last two sentences (''someone else had *got* Patrick Grady'' and ''She'd *scooped up* Patrick Grady'').

Like many of Trevor's stories, ''The Ballroom of Romance'' dramatizes its vision of alienation and disconnection through the theme of failed love; the story ends with Bridie's realization that her dreams are futile and that one day, to avoid having to live alone after her father's death, she probably will marry a man for whom she has no feeling. ''Teresa's Wedding,'' from Trevor's next collection of stories, *Angels at the Ritz*, relies on the same theme while focusing more directly on the institution of marriage. And although this theme is developed through a plot that is, in outline, thoroughly conventional – a story about two young people forced to marry after the girl becomes pregnant –

the story's use of realistic, ironically charged details, multiple centers of consciousness, and ironic juxtaposition make it one of the most effective of Trevor's stories in this vein.

The story operates chiefly through ironic contrasts between the conventional association of weddings with love and promise and the realities of the marriage between Teresa and Arty Cornish. The opening sets up this tension by means of a series of specific details that seem objectively described but in fact carry considerable ironic weight:

> The remains of the wedding-cake was on top of the piano in Swanton's lounge-bar, beneath a framed advertisement for Power's whiskey. Chas Flynn, the best man, had opened two packets of confetti: it lay thickly on the remains of the wedding-cake, on the surface of the bar and the piano, on the table and the two small chairs that the lounge-bar contained, and on the tattered green and red linoleum.[9]

This atmosphere of shabby futility is developed further by means of a roving point of view that, like a camera, sweeps through the lounge-bar, picking up images of moral debris and dipping in and out of various consciousnesses. The mother of the bride, Mrs Atty, is seen standing in a flowered dress "that blended easily with the confetti" (p. 132); the two fathers are at the bar, drinking whiskey urgently and trying to mask their uneasiness and displeasure by talking about greyhound racing; the local priest, who brought about the marriage, is also drinking whiskey, and talking to a woman who "sipped Winter's Tale sherry" (p. 132); the groom is drinking stout with his friends, one of whom works in the town's bacon factory and the other of whom serves behind the counter in the local hardware store and is known, accordingly, as "Screw Doyle"; Teresa is with her friends, one of whom, Philomena, plans to marry the local vet. The characterization of Philomena exemplifies how Trevor, in moving briefly into the consciousness of a minor character, is constantly working to develop the story's central contrast between romance and realism, illusion and irony. Philomena, the narrator says, "had every hope of marrying and had even planned her dress, in light lemony lace, with a Limerick veil," but when she thinks specifically of her intended, a note of unconscious irony and acquiescence, very close to that on which "The Ballroom of Romance" concludes, enters the narrative:

''and even if he was a few years older than he might be and had a car that smelt of cattle disinfectant, there was more to be said for Des Foley than for many another'' (p. 134).

The pathetic, forced jollity of Teresa's wedding celebration contains its own implicit contrast with what wedding parties are supposed to be like, but the events of this day are also frequently played off against the sordid details of the circumstances that led to the marriage, producing a more sharply and explicitly ironic undercurrent that depends on juxtapositions between past and present:

> 'God go with you, girl,' Father Hogan said to Teresa, motioning Kitty Roche and Philomena away. 'Isn't it a grand thing that's happened, Teresa?' His red-skinned face, with the shiny false teeth so evenly arrayed in it, was close to hers. For a moment she thought he might kiss her, which of course was ridiculous, Father Hogan kissing anyone, even at a wedding celebration.
>
> 'It's a great day for all of us, girl.'
>
> When she'd told her mother, her mother said it made her feel sick in her stomach. Her father hit her on the side of the face.
>
> (pp. 140–1)

''Teresa's Wedding'' also dramatizes its theme of alienation and futility through an essentially circular narrative shape. The story begins with the image of the confetti, moves around the enclosed, tattered surroundings of the lounge-bar, and comes to rest, at the end, on the image with which it opened, suggesting that this marriage, based on the forced acceptance of social convention rather than on love and free choice, is a trap from which there can be no exit. The only ''action'' in the story is internal, the destruction of what few illusions Teresa might have carried with her when she arrived at Swanton's lounge-bar to celebrate her wedding; after her husband of a few hours asks her to confirm or deny the claim of Screw Doyle to having once had sexual relations with her, Teresa is left with the same feeling of blank, necessary acquiescence that descends on Bridie at the end of ''The Ballroom of Romance'':

> At least they had no illusions, she thought. Nothing worse could happen than what had happened already, after Father Hogan had laid down the law. . . .

For a moment as Teresa stood there, the last moment before she left the lounge-bar, she felt that she and Artie might make some kind of marriage together because there was nothing that could be destroyed, no magic or anything else. He could ask her the question he had asked, while she stood there in her wedding dress: he could ask her and she could truthfully reply, because there was nothing special about the occasion, or the lounge-bar all covered in confetti.

(p. 143)

Both Bridie and Teresa are vicims of social forces over which they have little control – Bridie cannot abandon her father in the hills, and Teresa, given the nature of her community, has little choice but to marry Arty.[10]

"The Paradise Lounge" (*Beyond the Pale*) also examines failed love in the context of social alienation and disconnection in modern Ireland, and it does so by playing off against each other two limited points of view, each associated with an incomplete or frustrated love-affair: first, the largely physical extramarital relationship between the story's main center of consciousness, a young Irish woman named Beatrice, and her married lover, and second, the Platonic, largely fantasized relationship between an elderly woman, Miss Doheny, a resident of the provincial Irish town in which Beatrice and her lover stop for their last weekend fling, and a married man, Mr Meldrum, whom Miss Doheny has known, and quietly loved, most of her life. Each of the two women, upon seeing one another at a local pub known as the Paradise Lounge, misconstrues the nature of the other's relationship, and in so doing reveals the limitations of both their lives. Beatrice, having come to the anti-climactic conclusion of her exhausted relationship, romanticizes what she perceives to be the feelings between Miss Doheny and Mr Meldrum in a way that discloses the shortcomings of her character and of the sadly casual affair in which she no longer has any interest:

In this claustrophobic town, in this very lounge, there had been the endless lingering of a silent passion, startlingly different from the instant requiting of her own. . . .
He was loved, and in silence he returned that love. His plump, bespectacled wife had never had reason to feel betrayed; no shame or guilt attached. . . .

130

Yet the love that had continued for so long would go on now until the grave: without even thinking, Beatrice knew that that was so. The old woman paraded for a purpose the remnants of her beauty, the man was elegant in his tweed. How lovely that was! Beatrice thought, still muzzily surveying the people at the table, the wife who had not been deceived quite contentedly chatting, the two who belonged together occupying their magic worlds.[11]

The *naïveté* of Beatrice's attitude – suggested here in the ironies that resonate throughout the passage – is sharply, cruelly exposed at the end of the story, when the center of consciousness shifts to Miss Doheny; as Beatrice's misconceptions about Miss Doheny's relationship reveal her own weaknesses, so Miss Doheny's fantasies about the affair between Beatrice and her lover suggest the true nature of her relationship with Mr Meldrum – it is, in fact, closer to the world of Joyce's *Dubliners* than to the Platonic ideal imagined by Beatrice – and reveal a *naïveté* on her part that is at least the equal of Beatrice's:[12]

Miss Doheny passed through the darkened town, a familiar figure on a Saturday night. It had been the same as always, sitting there, close to him, the smoke drifting from the cigarette that lolled between his fingers. The girl by now would be close in a different way to the man who was somebody else's husband also. As in a film, their clothes would be scattered about the room that had been hired for love, their murmurs would break a silence. Tears ran through Miss Doheny's meticulous make-up, as often they did when she walked away from the Paradise Lounge on a Saturday night. It was difficult sometimes not to weep when she thought about the easy times that had come about in her lifetime, mocking the agony of her stifled love.

(p. 256)

Similar thematic preoccupations inform several of Trevor's short stories that have to do specifically with Protestant, Anglo-Irish Ireland, the Ireland to which Trevor is connected by birth. In these stories, Trevor, somewhat in the manner of Yeats, takes the decline of this once powerful class as an objective correlative for the loss of certain moral and cultural values in the twentieth century. But the stories need to be read principally in the light of

Trevor's governing concern with the tension between love and alienation, compassion and disconnection.

In "Mr McNamara" (*Angels at the Ritz*), an initiation story about a 13-year-old boy, the innocence and eventual disillusionment of the protagonist are connected closely to his being the oldest son in a prosperous but no longer grand Anglo-Irish family. As the boy realizes, the family, which runs a provincial mill and granary, is not what it once was – "As a family we belonged to the past. We were Protestants in what had become Catholic Ireland. We'd once been part of an ascendancy, but now it was not so" (p. 171) – but it suffers a sharper, more specifically moral decline in the course of the story. The sudden death of the boy's father, occuring the day after his thirteenth birthday, marks just the beginning of the boy's fall from innocence. The event that triggers the story's central moral epiphany comes more than a year later when the boy, increasingly obsessed with his father, bicycles to Dublin from his boarding-school to look up the mysterious Mr McNamara, supposedly his father's bar-room companion during his occasional business trips to Dublin, and a man who, because of the many stories about him that his father used to bring back to the family, has become a vivid part of the boy's imagination and of the life of his family. Thus, the discovery that Mr McNamara is, in fact, a woman is charged with an irony that dismantles the boy's faith in familial love and loyalty. But the story's final irony cuts even deeper. The boy's most devastating epiphany is the realization that he will never be able to tell his mother and sisters what he has learned, and that he is, therefore, a victim of his father's deceit and betrayal, an involuntary inheritor of moral wrong. The story's conclusion registers this painful realization with a forceful, first-person directness:

I watched my mother smile that Christmas morning, and I wanted to tell the truth because the truth was neat and without hypocrisy: I wanted carefully to say that I was glad my father was dead.

Instead I left the breakfast table and went to my bedroom. I wept there, and then washed my face in cold water from the jug on my wash-stand. I hated the memory of him and how he would have been that Christmas morning; I hated him for destroying everything. It was no consolation to me then that he had tried to share with us a person he loved in a way that was different from the way he loved us. I could neither forgive nor understand. I felt only bitterness that I, who had taken his place, must now continue his deception, and keep the secret of his lies and his hypocrisy.

(p. 186)

"The Wedding in the Garden" (*The News from Ireland*), another story with an Anglo-Irish setting, singles out class consciousness as a force of moral deceit and hypocrisy, and so a destroyer of love and connection. The story's plot is something of a commonplace in Irish fiction: a young Catholic maid named Dervla, working in a provincial hotel run by a prominent Protestant family, attracts the attentions of the young man of the household, named Christopher, then is forced by Christopher's mother to reject him as beyond her social standing, and finally must stand by helplessly as he marries into his own class. This narrative frame embodies an irony of circumstance that serves Trevor's purposes well; on the most basic level, Dervla's memories of her clandestine meetings with Christopher in one of the hotel's empty rooms are ironically played off against her presence, at the end of the story, as a maid at Christopher's wedding. This is compounded by ironies of character; it is Christopher's – and his entire class's – sense of honor that compels him to make good his family's promise to allow Dervla to remain in the family's employ for as long as she wants, even after Christopher sees that her presence may well destroy his marriage. It is also this sense of honor that forces Christopher to deceive his new wife, to keep from her his past relationship with Dervla.

Not until the very end of the story does Trevor unveil the cruellest irony of all, and he does so in a way thoroughly characteristic of the best of his writing. Throughout the story, the principal center of consciousness is Dervla, the victim of the class system. But in the story's final scene, the wedding celebration in the garden of the hotel, the center of consciousness shifts to Christopher, who realizes only too late the trap that he is in – that simply by being there, Dervla will always remind him of the price that he must pay for sacrificing love to social convention, and of the moral bankruptcy of his entire class and way of life:

He watched her walking away and was left again with the

insistence in her eyes. As the dining-room maid, she would become part of another family growing up in the hotel. . . . For all his life he would daily look upon hers, but no words would ever convey her undramatic revenge because the right to speak, once his gift to her, had been taken away. He had dealt in cruelty and so now did she: her gift to him, held over until his wedding day, was that afternoon shadows would gather for ever in Room 14, while she kept faith.[13]

Like "Mr McNamara," Trevor's novella *Nights at the Alexandra* is essentially an initiation story centering on a young Protestant boy. The setting for this narrative, however, differs sharply from the bucolic, semi-Edenic backgrounds of "Mr McNamara" and "The Wedding in the Garden"; the father of the young narrator of *Nights at the Alexandra* is the proprietor of a timberyard in a grubby provincial town, a rough-and-ready man who has worked his way up from low origins – "We were a Protestant family of the servant class which had come up in the world," the narrator, named Harry, says[14] – and whose manners and behavior are indistinguishable from those of many lower-class provincial Catholics. For Harry, his father, his family, the family business, the town itself all constitute a trap as deadening as any confronting the youthful narrators in Joyce's *Dubliners*:

. . . the timberyard and my father's ubiquitous presence in it, the endless whine of the saws, mud pitched up from the wheels of lorries, the rattle of rain on corrugated iron, the bitter odour of resin: that prospect appalled me, and I knew that what would accompany it within my self was the sullenness that had developed in my sister. . . . I dreaded the day when the hall-door would close behind both of us, when we would walk the few yards together to the timberyard, my sister Annie arriving later because the accounts shed didn't open until nine. . . . At one o'clock I would return over the same few yards with my father and my sister, and my father would hold forth while we ate boiled bacon or chops.

(pp. 32–3)

Against this world of drabness and routine, the elegant, mysterious life of the newly arrived Messengers – the wife an Englishwoman, the husband a German – stands in sharp contrast, and draws Harry to Cloverhill, the comfortable, spacious house on the edge of town where the Messengers take up residence. Moreover, the Messengers seem, especially in contrast to Harry's mother and father, very much in love, despite a relatively large difference in age and a potentially divisive difference in nationality. (The story is set during the Second World War, and the Messengers have come to Ireland because Frau Messenger could not live in Hitler's Germany, and Herr Messenger could not live in England.)

Harry's hopes of realizing the vague but powerful ambitions inspired by his relationship with the Messengers, especially with the young and elegant Frau Messenger, are shattered when he discovers that Frau Messenger is dying, and this realization marks a decided fall from innocence for Harry. But the story does not rest there. It maintains a delicate and, for Trevor, characteristic balance between disillusionment and hope, resignation and determination, alienation and connection. In her last months, Frau Messenger asks her husband to build a grand, luxurious movie house for the little town, and this building, named Alexandra for her, stands both as a symbol of Herr Messenger's love for his wife (". . . he was offering her a gift which was to be created as she wished, to bring pleasure to strangers" (p. 40)), and as a gesture of connection, of the selfless impulse to reach out beyond the confines of one's individual or intimate life, and "bring pleasure," as Harry puts it, to other people.

This balance between what the movie house represents and the counter-pointing significance of Frau Messenger's death is also embodied in Harry's character. The story of the Messengers and the movie house is told inside a narrative frame in which Harry, now 58, is recalling his youth.[15] Cloverhill has long since been boarded up, and the Alexandra, bequeathed to Harry years ago, is no longer in business. From one point of view, Harry has become a figure of alienation and loneliness, a man who has no children, who never married, who lives on the edge of society. "I am pitied because I am solitary and withdrawn," he says, "because I have not taken my place and am left in the end with nothing" (p. 80). But from Harry's own, subjective point of view, his life looks very different, very much less impoverished. He has his memories of the Messengers, his imagination, and, most important, his faith, however tarnished by the events that have occurred, in the power of love and connection:

> It is sad that through a quirk of fashion no one came much to
> the Alexandra these last few years. It is sad that rats are in
> charge at Cloverhill. But a husband's love and a woman's
> gratitude for sanctuary have not surrendered their potency. I am
> a fifty-eight-year-old cinema proprietor without a cinema, yet
> when I sit among the empty seats memory is enough. She smiles
> from the green-striped cushions, he spreads his drawings on the
> floor. My rain-soaked clothes drip on to the fender by the fire,
> there is happiness in spite of death and war. Fate has made me
> the ghost of an interlude; once in a while I say that in the town,
> trying to explain.
>
> (p. 80)

This passage, which concludes the novella, also strongly
encourages the consideration of Harry as an authorial figure. He
is, of course, the teller of this tale about the power and frailty of
love, but, more generally, he can be seen as a model of the
contemporary writer as Trevor perceives him – alienated from his
community (indeed, considered more than a little mad), but
strengthened by an inner faith that depends on imagination and,
above all, committed to "trying to explain."

All three of these narratives having to do with Anglo-Irish,
Protestant Ireland take Trevor out from the shadow of Joyce. But
even in recent stories more closely tied to the world of Joyce's
fiction, there is evidence that Trevor has come to some kind of
terms with this powerful ghost. Only a writer who is more or less
free from the anxiety of influence could, for example, have written
"Two More Gallants" (*The News from Ireland*), a story that is
essentially an extension of Joyce's "Two Gallants." (In Trevor's
version, it is a Joycean scholar rather than a Joycean character
who is made the victim of a scheme of deceit.) And in one of the
most accomplished stories in *The News from Ireland*, "Music," the
protagonist quite self-consciously identifies himself with Joyce,
especially with Joyce's decision to leave Ireland.

"Music" opens in a voice that is distinctly, overtly Joycean:

> At thirty-three Justin Condon was a salesman of women's
> undergarments, regularly traversing five counties with his
> samples and his order book in a Ford Fiesta. He had obediently

accepted this role, agreeing when his father had suggested it to
him. His father in his day had been a commercial traveller also
and every Friday Justin returned to the house his father had
returned to, arriving at much the same hour and occupying a
room he had in childhood shared with his three brothers.

(p. 226)

The parallels suggested here between Justin and Little Chandler,
of Joyce's "A Little Cloud," are furthered through Justin's
fantasies about getting free of his job, which he sees as a threat
to his career as a musician, and about getting out of Ireland.
Moreover, because these fantasies are centered specifically around
Joyce himself, Joyce, in effect, plays the role of Gallaher, the
"successful" journalist in "A Little Cloud," to Justin's Little
Chandler. This blatantly self-conscious use of Joyce and his
characters suggests the extent to which Trevor, at this point in his
writing, is confident about his relationship to Joyce, and about his
ability to clear his own ground. And, like many of the stories
discussed earlier, "Music" bears the distinctive imprint of
Trevor's style and vision. Justin's illusions about his musical
abilities – paralleling Little Chandler's fantasies about his gifts as
a poet – are not merely the pathetic product of a life of quiet
desperation, but the result of a calculated deceit on the part of
other human beings, and a keenly self-interested exploitation of
Justin's innocence . As Justin realizes only too late, the local priest
and the woman whom he thinks of as Aunt Roche have encouraged his piano-playing only as a means to create situations in
which they could be together. And so Justin is more than a victim
of a vaguely paralyzing social environment from which he feels the
need to escape, as Little Chandler does; he is the victim of a moral
corruption that is quite specifically embodied in human character,
and for which distinct human responsibility can be assigned. "He
had clutched at the straw they had offered him and it had kept
him going," Justin thinks near the end of the story. "He had
played his part, not knowing what it was, offering them a straw
also: for the first time, he realized that" (p. 247).

As Trevor himself has said, the contemporary Irish writer has
more to contend with than Joyce's shadow. "In Ireland you can
escape neither politics nor history," he said in *A Writer's Ireland*,
"for when you travel through the country today the long conflict

137

its landscape has known does not as readily belong in the faraway past as Hastings or Stamford Bridge does for the English."[16] Trevor's writing about Ireland has increasingly taken cognizance of that long conflict, and of its disasterous manifestation in contemporary Ulster. But Trevor's fiction dealing with these issues never loses sight of the moral vision that informs the best of his work. In his short stories dealing with political and religious conflict in Ireland, and in *Fools of Fortune* and *The Silence in the Garden*, Ireland provides chiefly a backdrop – an unusually powerful and dramatic one – for an exploration of Trevor's broad thematic concerns. On the one hand, these narratives tend to see individual values like love and affection as threatened by pressures exerted by the past and by political and religious ideologies. On the other hand, Trevor's writing in this vein also insists on the need for moral responsibility, for a humanistic compassion that takes the form of commitments to people and principles that lie beyond the immediate confines of self and family.[17]

In at least one of Trevor's early stories with such concerns, the backdrop proves somewhat too dramatic. "The Distant Past" (*Angels at the Ritz*) relies on a straightforwardly before-and-after structure that works against complex characterization, and tends to ignore fine distinctions, moral and political. Set in a provincial town much like that of Trevor's non-political Irish fiction, the story turns on the relationship between an elderly Anglo-Irish, Protestant couple living out their years in shabby gentility and the local townspeople, most of them middle-class, Catholic, and more or less nationalistic. The story moves from a state of communal innocence, in which the Middletons and townspeople live in tolerance and even cordiality, to a state in which, after the news of the outbreak of violence in Ulster reaches the community, the relationship is poisoned, and a whole history of division and sectarian hatred surfaces.

Although this story fails to achieve the complexity and nuance of character and situation that define the best of Trevor's short stories, it does raise some of the major thematic issues that Trevor's writing in this vein is concerned with. It insists, for example, that the past cannot be discounted, that history almost always makes itself felt in the present, often, in Ireland at least, in tragic ways. It also tends to see individual values as threatened by history, and by ideological commitments. The following passage embodies both these ideas, at the same time that it reveals one characteristic – the tendency to rely on summary rather than on dramatization – that identifies the story as an early one of its kind:

> The Border was more than sixty miles away, but over that distance had spread some wisps of the fog of war. As anger rose in the town at the loss of fortune so there rose also the kind of talk there had been in the distant past. There was talk of atrocities and counter-atrocities, and of guns and gelignite and the rights of people. There was bitterness suddenly in Mrs Keogh's bar because of the lack of trade, and in the empty hotel there was bitterness also. . . .
>
> The Middletons naturally didn't discuss these rebuffs but they each of them privately knew that there was no conversation they could have at this time with the people of the town. The stand they had taken and kept to for so many years no longer seemed ridiculous in the town. Had they driven with a Union Jack now they would, astoundingly, have been shot.
>
> (pp. 39–40)

Like "The Distant Past," "Another Christmas" (*Lovers of Their Time*) measures the effects of the violence in Ulster on the private lives of individuals, but this story is more complex and ambitious, particularly in terms of its moral vision. When the central character, an Irishman named Dermot living in England with his wife, defends the bombings by the IRA in Northern Ireland on the ground that they constitute a legitimate response to centuries of discrimination against Catholics – the argument that has apparently alienated the couple's landlord and close friend, Mr Joyce – he is, whether right or wrong in terms of the political issues, acting as a kind of truth-teller, trying to force his wife to face the political and historical realities lying beyond the confines of everyday family life. "You have to state the truth," Dermot tells Norah, in response to her complaints about losing Mr Joyce's friendship.[18] Norah's answer clearly defines the other side of the issue: "I never yet cared for a North of Ireland person, Catholic or Protestant. Let them fight it out and not bother us" (p. 36).

At the end of the story, Trevor turns the question around. Shifting the center of consciousness to Norah, he brings to the emotional foreground the cost to individual feelings and values, especially to the love and affection necessary to a fulfilled marriage, of the kind of intense commitment to political ideology that Dermot has been arguing for. The closing of the story exemplifies admirably Trevor's ability, relying chiefly on irony, to hold these two positions in a careful, resonating balance; Norah suddenly realizes that the sacrificial victim is, in some ways, herself, and hearing her husband talking about Ulster and the obligation of Catholics to defend themselves, she sees only what she considers a streak of terrible cruelty in her husband, and realizes that she does not love him:

> He talked but she did not listen. He spoke of keeping faith with their own, of being a Catholic. Crime begot crime, he said, God wanted it to be known that one evil led to another. She continued to look at him while he spoke, pretending to listen but wondering instead if in twelve months' time, when another Christmas came, he would still be cycling from house to house to read gas meters. Or would people have objected, requesting a meter-reader who was not Irish? An objection to a man with an Irish accent was down-to-earth and ordinary. It didn't belong in the same grand category as crime begetting crime or God wanting something to be known, or in the category of truth and conscience. In the present circumstances the objection would be understandable and fair. It seemed even right that it should be made, for it was a man with an Irish accent in whom the worst had been brought out by the troubles that had come, who was guilty of a cruelty no one would have believed him capable of. Their harmless elderly landlord might die in the course of that same year, a friendship he had valued lost, his last Christmas lonely. Grand though it might seem in one way, all of it was petty.
>
> (pp. 37–8)

These counterpointed moral positions also inform two of Trevor's most accomplished short stories – both having to do with the violence in Ulster – "Attracta" (*Lovers of Their Time*) and the title story of *Beyond the Pale*. "Attracta" contains a particularly gruesome report from the front – the account of a young Englishwoman whose husband's head was mailed to her after he was killed while stationed in Belfast, and who then moved to Belfast and joined the Woman's Peace Movement only to be raped by seven men, and, in despair, finally killed herself – but it is a sub-plot, serving chiefly to trigger changes in the story's central character, an elderly Protestant schoolteacher living and working in a provincial Irish town similar to those in most of Trevor's Irish stories. When the schoolteacher, Attracta, named after an Irish saint of the fifth or sixth century, reads in the newspaper about the Englishwoman, Penelope Vade, she is inspired to face her own moral responsibilities as a teacher as well as her own and her community's history, a past marked by the same kind of violence and attempted forgiveness as characterize the Penelope Vade story. When Attracta was a child, during the Anglo-Irish war, her parents were killed accidentally in an ambush meant for the Black-and-Tans and organized by two townspeople, a Protestant named Mr Devereux and a Catholic woman, Geraldine Casey. Since that time, Mr Devereux and Geraldine Casey have tried to effect some kind of penance for what was done in the name of political ideology through acts of individual, personal kindness toward Attracta.

Attracta's perception of the parallels between these two stories – one recent, one in the past – leads to an act of moral courage, her own attempt to reach beyond the seemingly safe insularity of her private life and recognize connections to other people's worlds. This is the message of the speech that she delivers to her stunned schoolchildren – that such connections and such moral responsibilities exist. But in the end, her efforts, like those of other truth-tellers in Trevor's fiction, fail. Moreover, Attracta's attempts to enlighten her schoolchildren meet with rejection not because the children are too innocent, but because they are too experienced in the ways of a world dominated by alienation and disconnection. The Penelope Vade story does not shock them into new attitudes and moral commitments, as it shocked Attracta, because for them, hardened by overexposure to violence and terror, the story is not even disturbing. Trevor reveals this bleak vision by means of a shift to the children as a center of consciousness:

> To the children she appeared be talking now to herself. She was old, a few of them silently considered; that was it. She didn't appear to understand that almost every day there was the kind of vengeance she spoke of reported on the television. Bloodshed was wholesale, girls were tarred and left for dead, children no

older than they were armed with guns.

(p. 213)

Attracta does have the last word in the story, but it is one that is at least as doubting as it is affirming. When the center of consciousness shifts back to her, Attracta's sense of failure is only partly offset by her faith in the inherent value of telling the truth, a faith that characterizes several of Trevor's authorial figures:

> It had meant nothing when she'd said that people change. The gleam of hope she'd offered had been too slight to be of use, irrelevant in the horror they took for granted, as part of life. Yet she could not help still believing that it mattered when monsters did not remain monsters for ever. It wasn't much to put against the last bleak moments of Penelope Vade, but it was something for all that. She wished she could have made her point.

(pp. 213–14)

In the end, Attracta pays a high price – the loss of her job and her status in the community – for her attempt to tell the truth, just as Penelope Vade paid the much higher price of her own life for her attempt to respond to violence and hatred with forgiveness and compassion.

Like "Attracta," "Beyond the Pale" relies on the interplay between two plots to dramatize the conflict between political commitment and private values and, at the same time, to affirm the individual's moral responsibility to the world beyond the self. The sub-plot in this story, about a young Ulster woman killed by her former lover after she rejects him and begins making bombs in London for the IRA, is concerned not just with the violence in Northern Ireland, but also with the political and religious attitudes – the fanatical commitment to ideology – that lie behind the violence.

Structured around the same innocence–experience paradigm as that which governs "The Distant Past," the sub-plot of "Beyond the Pale" is handled with considerably more complexity and force than is the plot of the earlier story. For one thing, this account of fanaticism leading to death is indirectly narrated, first told by the murderer to a middle-aged Englishwoman named Cynthia, on holiday in Co. Antrim with her husband Strafe and their two friends Milly and Dekko, and then retold by Cynthia to her three

142

companions after the young man, apparently in despair, drowns himself in the sea in front of the hotel in which they all are staying. And Cynthia casts the story in precisely the moral terms that govern much of Trevor's Irish fiction, particularly the threat to individual values posed by political ideology. "He hated the violence that possessed her," Cynthia tells her puzzled audience, "yet he was full of it himself: he knew he couldn't betray her with anything but death. Humanity had left both of them when he visited her again in Maida Vale" (p. 103). Moreover, the significance of the young man's story lies ultimately less in itself than in its effects on Cynthia and her companions. It provokes Cynthia to a moral action, much as the Penelope Vade story provoked Attracta, and she takes on the role of truth-teller; in a long, disturbed monologue, she tries to make her husband and their friends see their inevitable connection with this world of violence that lies just beyond the false Eden of their hotel and morally just beyond the pale of their private lives. "All I am saying," she says at one point, "is that we should root our heads out of the sand and wonder about two people who are beyond the pale" (p. 104).[19] (Because the pale also refers to the area around Dublin that was for centuries the boundary of English governance in Ireland, and because Cynthia and her companions are English, the title of the story suggests another kind of political connection argued for in Cynthia's speech – between the English and the Irish.) On the level of private affairs, Cynthia also jolts her listeners with the revelation that she has known for years about the infidelity and hypocrisy, specifically the affair between Milly and Cynthia's husband, that have poisoned their lives together.

Like most of Trevor's truth-tellers, Cynthia is largely ignored. Her husband and her friends are convinced that the experience of talking to the young man has unhinged her, a typical response, in Trevor's fiction, to people who try to make others see the importance of moral responsibility and connection. The strength of the resistance to all that Cynthia is saying is felt powerfully in the story through the use of Milly rather than Cynthia as a first-person narrator. Milly embodies all that Cynthia's final speech is pitched against, all the qualities – indifference, smugness, ignorance – that stand in the way of compassion and connection. Moreover, through Milly's voice, Trevor is able to bring into play a counterpointing irony; at the same time that Milly's strong, unchanging presence in the story suggests that the values and attitudes that she represents are not easily overcome, her voice, through ironic overstatement and juxtaposition, works to subvert much of what she stands for. The effects of this can be seen, for example, in Milly's reflections about the violence in Ulster:

> People in England thought us mad of course: they see so much of the troubles on television that it's naturally difficult for them to realize that most places are just as they've always been. Yet coming as we did, taking the road along the coast, dawdling through Ballygally, it was impossible to believe that somewhere else the unpleasantness was going on. We'd never seen a thing, nor even heard people talking about incidents that might have taken place. It's true that after a particularly nasty carry-on a few winters ago we did consider finding somewhere else, in Scotland perhaps, or Wales. But as Strafe put it at the time, we felt we owed a certain loyalty to the Malseeds and indeed to everyone we'd come to know round about, people who'd always been glad to welcome us back. It seemed silly to lose our heads, and when we returned the following summer we knew immediately we'd been right.
>
> (pp. 79–80)

The tone of this passage both perfectly characterizes and ironically undermines Milly. The euphemisms, for example – "the unpleasantness," "incidents," "a particularly nasty carry-on" – reveal a willed innocence, a reductive smugness that rules out any understanding of the world beyond that of the self. And the phrase "It seemed silly to lose our heads" not only underscores this *naïveté*, but also, by the end of the story, rebounds on all of them in the presumed madness of Cynthia and the disruption of their carefully managed peace and security.

Although Cynthia is given a forum for her truth-telling, the last word in the story belongs to Milly. And despite a vague realization that something, somehow, has been changed, Milly's voice shows few signs of having been seriously affected by what Cynthia has been saying:

> Cynthia stumbled off, leaving a silence behind her. Before it was broken I knew she was right when she said we would just go home, away from this country we had come to love. And I knew

as well that neither here nor at home would she be led to a blue
van that was not quite an ambulance. Strafe would stay with
her because Strafe is made like that, honourable in his own
particular way. I felt a pain where perhaps my heart is, and
again I wanted to cry. Why couldn't it have been she who had
gone down to the rocks and slipped on the seaweed or just
walked into the sea, it didn't matter which? Her awful rigmarole
hung about us as the last of the tea things were gathered up –
the earls who'd fled, the famine and the people planted. The
children were there too, grown up into murdering riff-raff.

(p. 109)

The passage is full of the unconscious irony that undercuts Milly's
voice throughout the story: Strafe, although he has been exposed
as an adulterer, can still be considered "honourable in his own
particular way"; Milly feels a pain "where *perhaps* my heart is";
she grieves not for the terrible waste of human life and potential
caused by what is going on just past the borders of the hotel
grounds, but for the loss of her own serenity and complacency;
and the Irish can be dismissed as nothing but "murdering riff-
raff." This is the voice of everything that Trevor, in his efforts to
convey a humanistic vision of moral responsibility, is writing
against; but it is also, given Trevor's realistic vision of the contemporary world, a voice that must be – as it is here – given its due.

In three important recent works, the long title story of *The News
from Ireland* and the novels *Fools of Fortune* and *The Silence in the
Garden*, Trevor has turned to a more markedly historical perspective to explore some of these moral issues. "The News from
Ireland" uses the Great Famine of the late 1840s to portray
history as a web in which individuals struggle, usually without
success, to maintain some kind of control over their lives. At the
same time, although political and religious ideologies are portrayed
as potentially anti-humanistic, this story about the life of a Protestant, Anglo-Irish estate during the dark days of the famine affirms
the responsibility of the individual to connect meaningfully with
the world of public events lying beyond the self.[20]

The story is built around a contrast between two characters and
their perspectives – one, the Protestant butler Fogarty, who
embodies the bitterness born of strongly held political and religious
views, and the other, a young English governess named Anna

145

THE IRISH FICTION

Maria Heddoe, in Ireland for the first time and innocent in a number of ways. Fogarty's inability to see beyond the blinding attitudes generated by ideology is dramatized in his views of the new English family, the Pulvertafts of Ipswich, who have come to live in the house. In the eyes of Fogarty, who has been a servant in the house most of his life, the Pulvertafts, no matter what their motives and what they do to try to relieve the suffering of their starving tenants, can never be accepted, because they are not Irish: "Serving them in the dining-room, holding for them a plate of chops or hurrying to them a gravy dish, he wishes he might speak the truth as it appears to him: that their fresh, decent blood is the blood of the invader though they are not themselves invaders, that they perpetuate theft without being thieves" (p. 10). Like all the characters in the story, Fogarty is both a product of history and a victim of it; the events of the past have twisted him into a figure of alienation and disconnection. At the end of the story, he is given a moment as a kind of truth-teller, but the truth that he tells is only that of his distorted vision. In a lengthy monologue delivered to Anna Maria, he predicts a future for Ireland that lamentably came true, but the qualities of bitterness and fanaticism that make him a reliable prophet of Ireland's future also sharply define his limitations as a moral guide and a human being:

> He told me of a dream he'd had the night before or last week, I was too upset to note which. The descendants of the people who had been hungry were in the dream, and the son of George Arthur Pulvertaft was shot in the hall of the house, and no Pulvertaft lived in the place again. The road that had been laid in charity was overgrown through neglect, and the gardens were as they had been at the time of old Hugh Pulvertaft, their beauty strangled as they returned to wildness.
>
> (p. 44)

The story turns on a confrontation between Fogarty and Anna Maria, an outsider as well as a figure of innocence, and the consequent changes in Anna Maria's character – specifically, in her having to come to terms with the realities of death and disease that lie just outside the door of the Big House. The story's final shift to Fogarty as center of consciousness describes this accurately, despite the ever-present tinge of bitterness in his mind: "It is she, not he, who came from England and was distressed. She has wept into her pillow, she has been sick at heart. Stranger and visitor, she has written in her diary the news from Ireland. Stranger and visitor, she has learnt to live with things" (p. 46). But what Fogarty cannot see, because of his own fanatical blindness, is that Anna Maria, in losing the innocence that she brought with her, has done more than simply learn to live with things. Much of the story consists of the diary that Fogarty refers to, and this document reveals a growing understanding of what is happening outside:

> I lay there thinking of the starvation, of the faces of the silent women when they come to the gate-lodge for food. There is a yellow-greyness in the flesh of their faces, they are themselves like obedient animals. Their babies die when they feed them grass and roots; in their arms at the gate-lodge the babies who survive are silent also, too weak to cry until the sustenance they receive revives them. Last night I lay thinking of the men who are turned away from the work on the road because they have not the strength that is necessary. I thought of the darkness in the cottages, of dawn bringing with it the glaring eyes of death. I thought of the graves again clawed open, the earth still loose, another carcass pushed on to the rotting heap.
>
> (p. 37)

This understanding carries with it an implied sense of moral responsibility and compassion, a belief in the need for connection with the world outside the intimate life of the family – attitudes that need to be distinguished sharply from the anti-humanistic political and religious prejudices of Fogarty.

FOOLS OF FORTUNE

The innocence–experience paradigm visible in the contrast between Anna Maria and Fogarty in "The News from Ireland" is developed, in *Fools of Fortune*, into a full-scale tragedy that represents in many ways the most accomplished of Trevor's novels.[21] At the center of this novel about the demise of a Protestant, Anglo-Irish family is the tension between history and the individual, between political ideology and personal values, between the unhappy legacy of Ireland's political past and the love of an Anglo-Irishman for his English cousin. It is a tension, moreover, that can only be resolved, given "the weight of circumstances" that presses on all the characters, in a tragic way. The central relationship in the book – between the Anglo-Irish Willie Quinton and his distant English cousin, Marianne Woodcombe – is played out against a powerful backdrop of political and historical events that eventually force Willie to sacrifice his love and take on a role more or less thrust upon him by forces over which he has little control. At the same time that the novel measures, in these ways, the costs to human love exacted by political commitment, it also insists on the individual's moral responsibility to act as Willie acts, to recognize an obligation larger than that to one other human being.

The history that provides the force of tragic inevitability in this novel begins not just with the burning of the Quinton's Big House in Co. Cork during the Anglo-Irish war – in some ways, the central event of the book – but much farther back, at least as far back as the Great Famine of the 1840s when another Woodcombe from Dorset, Anna, married Willie's great-grandfather and soon thereafter found herself, as does Marianne almost a century later, entangled in the web of Irish history. Although the action of the novel begins in 1918 and ends in 1982, Anna Quinton is never far from the surface of the book, and her story, woven into the fabric of the novel's fictional present, embodies the same tension between individual freedom and public responsibility as dramatized in the Willie-Marianne plot. As the burning of Kilneagh destroyed Willie's family and led to his own alienating crime of revenge, so Anna's fierce political commitment to the cause of the famine victims brought about her alienation from her family in England: "*You spread calumny over our name*, her irate father wrote. *Since you will not cease in your absurd charges against this country, I have no choice left but to disown you*" (p. 35).

Willie is told this story in his childhood, and the strength of Anna's commitment, and the price that she paid for it, are embedded in his character. The chain of tragic events that lead to disaster in Willie's and Marianne's lives is set off by precisely the kind of morally motivated act that characterized Anna's efforts to do something about the famine. All the main events of the novel – the execution of Doyle, a Kilneagh employee found hung from a tree with his tongue cut out, the usual punishment for informers; the burning of Kilneagh, and the deaths of Willie's father and two sisters, at the hands of the Black-and-Tans, presumably in response to the killing of Doyle; the subsequent alcoholism and suicide of Willie's mother; and finally, Willie's killing of Sergeant Rudkin, the man believed to be responsible for burning Kilneagh – are triggered by the decision of Willie's father, an Anglo-Irish Protestant, to support the revolutionary leader Michael Collins.

Through all these events, including those that take control of Marianne's and Willie's lives, runs a streak of tragic inevitability, a sense that the events of history have a life of their own that cannot be denied or ignored. This is the point of several of Marianne's diary entries, looking back over the seemingly bewildering series of events that have made a mockery of her love for Willie and of Willie's dreams of a life that would happily follow the pattern of his father's:

> *I had never even heard of the Battle of the Yellow Ford until Father Kilgarriff told me. . . . Just another Irish story it had seemed to you and perhaps, if ever you think of it, it still does. But the battlefield continuing is part of the pattern I see everywhere around me, as your exile is also. How could we in the end have pretended? How could we have rebuilt Kilneagh and watched our children playing among the shadows of destruction? The battlefield has never quietened.*
>
> (pp. 211–12)

> *Father Kilgarriff died today, no trouble in his great old age. He was right when he said that there's not much left in a life when murder has been committed. That moment when I guessed the truth in Mr Lanigan's office; that moment when she opened the secret drawer; that moment when he stood at his mother's bedroom door and saw her dead. After each brief moment there was as little chance for any one of us as there was for Kilneagh after the soldier's wrath. Truncated lives, creatures of the shadows. Fools of fortune, as his father would have said; ghosts we became.*
>
> (pp. 233–4)

The innocence–experience paradigm is essential to the expression of this tragic vision of human beings as fools of fortune. The impingement of political and religious fanaticism, with its roots in Ireland's long divisive history, on the peaceful world of Kilneagh destroys the innocence of the young Willie just as, in "The News from Ireland," the famine explodes the innocence of Anna Maria. This framework is introduced early in *Fools of Fortune*, in Willie's lyrical, Edenic memories of Kilneagh as it once was, and in his naive childhood belief that the future could be counted on to repeat the perceived tranquillity of the present:

> I knew that one day I would inherit this mill. I liked the thought of that, of going to work there, of learning what my father had had to learn about grain and the machinery that ground it. I liked the mill itself, its grey stone softened with Virginia creeper, the doors of lofts and stores a reddish brown, paint that over the years had lost its shine due to the sun; in a central gable the green-faced clock was always a minute fast. I loved the smell of the place, the warm dry smell of corn, the cleanness even though there was dust in the air. I enjoyed watching the huge wheel turning in the mill-race, one cog engaging the next. The timber of the chutes was smooth with wear, leather flaps opening and falling back, then opening again. The sacks had *Quinton* on them, the letters of our name arranged in a circle.
>
> (pp. 19–20)

It is a long way from these pre-lapsarian memories – conveyed in part by the passage's languid rhythms and its imagery of smoothness, roundness, and repetition – to the nightmare world of everything that descends on Willie from the time that Kilneagh is burnt to the ground. One reliable barometer of the distance that the novel travels between the poles of innocence and experience is the difference between the young Willie, as portrayed in this passage and others like it, and the daughter of his short-lived union with Marianne, the disturbed Imelda. As the fruit of that union, Imelda represents, on one level, the troubled relationship between England and Ireland – a parallel suggested by Marianne's mother's remark "that when you looked at the map Ireland and England seemed like lovers" (pp. 202–3). Moreover, the nature of Imelda's illness, particularly her self-centered obsessions with the past and with violence, embodies the notion that history cannot be ignored. Trevor frequently relies on unbalanced characters – Mrs Eckdorf and Miss Gomez, for example, or Matilda, in "Matilda's England" – to reveal important truths, and Imelda's hallucinations about the killing of Sergeant Rudkin and the burning of Kilneagh vividly dramatize, and with the striking psychological realism observable in other characters of this type in Trevor's fiction, this view:

> She closed her eyes and in the room above the vegetable shop
> blood spurted in a torrent, splashing on to the wallpaper that
> was torn and hung loosely down. The blood was sticky, running
> over the backs of her hands and splashing on to her hair. It
> soaked through her clothes, warm when it reached her skin.
>
> Imelda pressed her face into the nettles and did not feel their
> stinging. She pressed her fists into her ears. She closed her eyes
> as tightly as she could.
>
> But nothing went away.
>
> The screaming of the children began, and the torment of the
> flames on their flesh. The dogs were laid out dead in the yard,
> and the body of the man in the teddy-bear dressing-gown lay
> smouldering on the stairs. The blood kept running on her
> hands, and was tacky in her hair.
>
> (pp. 218–19)

The tragic curve of *Fools of Fortune* is not, however, so relentless
as all this suggests. At the end of the novel, after Willie and
Marianne have paid the inevitable price for Willie's political
actions and commitments, Willie returns – an old man now – to
Kilneagh, where Marianne has remained, raising Imelda as best
she could. And although the last few years that Willie and
Marianne have together fall far short of what they once envisioned
as their future, there is none the less an affirmative circularity to
the book that resists somewhat the tragic implications of its general
design. This is most specifically suggested in the way that the tranquillity of the opening pages of the novel, describing Willie's
memories of Kilneagh when he was a boy, are echoed at the
book's end, perhaps most vividly in the character of Imelda. Once
tortured by hallucinations of a bloody and violent past, at the end
of the book Imelda's consciousness settles on precisely those
Edenic scenes from Willie's childhood memories with which the
book began:

> Her happiness is like a shroud miraculously about her, its
> source mysterious except to her. No one but Imelda knows that
> in the scarlet drawing-room wood blazes in the fireplace while
> the man of the brass log-box reaches behind him for the hand
> of the serving-girl. Within globes like onions, lights dimly

gleam, and carved on the marble of the mantelpiece the clustered leaves are as delicate as the flicker of the flames. No one knows that she is happiest of all when she stands in the centre of the Chinese carpet, able to see in the same moment the garden and the furniture of the room, and to sense that yet another evening is full of the linnet's wings.

(p. 238)

Imelda's thoughts here (including the allusion to Yeats's "The Lake Isle of Innisfree") represent an affirmation of the power of love and the imagination to stand up to the tragic curve of events generated by history and political ideology.

The strikingly lyrical quality of the writing about love in this novel has much the same effect. The description of the night of Imelda's conception, for example, knows no equal in Trevor's fiction for its subjective, emotional intensity; it is given in Marianne's first-person voice, and describes the night after the death of Willie's mother, the event that eventually drives Willie to the act of revenge that cuts him off from Marianne:

I waited downstairs for an hour or so, but it was much later, when I was undressing in my bedroom, that I heard your footfall on the stairs, which seemed like fate also. I pulled my nightdress over my head and slipped into the cold bed. I wept immediately. Had we been together now, would I have put my arms about you, and drawn your head on to my breast to kiss away your suffering? And would you have forgiven me for the accident of my English birth? For an hour or more I lay there wretchedly, and then I rose and lifted the paraffin lamp from its shelf.

I did not knock, even lightly, on the panels of your door but opened it instead. All judgment had gone from me, all fear and rectitude. I cared about nothing except that you should know I loved you, that you might find at least some comfort in knowing it. I placed the lamp on your dressing-table and spoke your name.

(pp. 138–9)

This passage also exemplifies how the narrative structure of the book – one different from those employed in any other of Trevor's novels – works to convey the force of the feelings between Willie and Marianne. The book is divided into separate sections attributed to Willie, Marianne, and Imelda, and with the exception of Imelda's brief narratives, they are written in the first person; the result is that the usual mix of objectivity and ambiguity generated by the use of multiple perspectives is substantially tempered by the subjectivity and intimacy of the first-person point of view. More generally, the shift to a highly impressionistic style from time to time dramatizes the conflict between history and the individual, particularly the notion of history as impinging on individual freedom and values. The burning of Kilneagh is perhaps the most notable instance of this; the event is described entirely from Willie's innocent, confused point of view, and the impressionistic quality of the writing calls attention to the ways in which events outside the individual invade and disrupt the private space of consciousness:

I awoke with a tickling in my nostrils. I lay there, knowing that something was different, not sure what it was. There was a noise, like the distant rushing of wind in trees.

Too drowsy to wonder properly, I slept again. There were voices calling out, and the screaming of my sisters, and the barking of the dogs. The rushing noise was closer. 'Willie! Willie!' Tim Paddy shouted.

I was in Tim Paddy's arms, and then there was the dampness of the grass before the pain began, all over my legs and back. The ponies and my mother's horse snorted and neighed. I could hear their hooves banging at the stable doors.

There were stars in the sky. An orange glow crept over the edges of my vision. The noise there'd been had changed, becoming a kind of crackling, with crashes that sounded like thunder. I couldn't move. I thought: We are all like this, Geraldine and Deirdre, my mother and father, Josephine and Mrs Flynn; we are lying on the wet grass, in pain. . . .

Through the fever of this nightmare floated the two portraits in the drawing-room, my dog-faced great grandfather and plain, merciful Anna Quinton. I seemed to be in the drawing-room myself, gathering up my school books and placing them in the corner cupboard. After that I was in the dog-cart, asking my father why Father Kilgarriff had been unfrocked. I saw that the teeth glistening in the confessional were Anna Quinton's, which was why Father Kilgarriff read her letters. I would understand such things, my father said, when I went away to school; that was why I had to. . . .

There were further gunshots and one by one the dogs stopped barking. The horse and the ponies must have been released because I heard them galloping somewhere. Something touched my leg, the edge of a boot, I thought. It grazed the pain, but I knew that I must not call out. I knew what Josephine had implied when she'd whispered to be still. The men who were walking away must not be seen; they had been seen by O'Neill and Tim Paddy, who must have come up from the gate-lodge. My eyes were closed, and what I saw in the darkness was Geraldine's drawing of Doyle hanging from the tree, the flames of the drawing-room making a harmless black crinkle of it.

(pp. 51–3)

Willie's thoughts here also place this event in the historical context that is so crucial to the book's tragic design. The flashback to Anna Quinton and the glimpsed memory of Willie's sister's picture of the man hanged for being an informer bring to the foreground the chain of events that have led to this night, and also forecast another chain of events leading away from it into a tragically determined future.

Although *Fools of Fortune* is not without its flaws – the long section describing Willie's experiences at boarding-school seems slightly self-indulgent – it is arguably the most accomplished of Trevor's novels, in terms of its characterization of Willie and Marianne, of its thematic exploration of the connection between history and the individual, of its formal achievements, particularly its combination of multiple perspectives and first-person narration, and, finally, of the sheer quality of its prose. The following passage, for example, describing Marianne wandering the streets of Cork, carrying Willie's child and looking for some trace of her vanished lover, is characterized by a power of sensual evocation, a psychological authenticity, and a formal complexity – particularly in the subtle movement between action and reflection – that argue for Trevor's status as a master of prose fiction:

I passed the shop windows we had passed together, the Turkish delight shop, the façade of the Victoria Hotel, brightly lit. I remembered the beggarwoman you had so harshly turned away, and the seagulls above our heads. By the river it was bitterly cold. In the sunshine of that summer we'd watched the men painting the ironwork of their cargo vessels. We'd lingered on all our walks.

Darkly the river slurped now, an oily sheen gleaming in the moonlight. Had I been absurd, when that summer was over, to imagine in the rectory and at school that we might be married? I had imagined so very clearly your mother and your aunts in the church, my father guiding us through the service, my wedding dress with a shade of yellow in it. We would sing Psalm 23, I'd thought, and afterwards we would be together for ever.

Slowly I walked along the quay. What courage your mother had possessed to draw a sleeve back and expose those vulnerable arteries throbbing beneath the skin, to take the blade from the coloured paper that wrapped it, to bear the pain, the sliver of metal slipping home. In a month or so the condition of my body would be apparent to everyone who saw me; I could not melt away as you and Josephine had. I wished you might know that I stood above the cold river, but I knew I would not be granted even that. And then I wished I had your mother's courage.

(pp. 177–8)

THE SILENCE IN THE GARDEN

If the ghost of Yeats is to be glimpsed from time to time in the pages of *Fools of Fortune* – and the occasionally elegaic tone of that novel as well as its setting certainly call it to mind – Yeats's presence is at least as powerful in Trevor's most recent novel, *The Silence in the Garden* (1988). The principal focus of this book is a once powerful Anglo-Irish Protestant family that has been living in Ireland in gentility if not splendor since the seventeenth century, and the plot is chiefly concerned with charting the decline of this family during the tumultuous early decades of this century.

This novel, and *Fools of Fortune*, are Yeatsian, however, only on the surface. Their concern with the plight of the Anglo-Irish in the twentieth century has little to do with a lament for the passing of high cultural values in a world of greasy-till materialism. Rather, the collapse of this class that once governed almost every aspect of Irish life is used in both novels to dramatize Trevor's concern with the relationship between past and present, with the ways in which history, and indeed the whole world of public events, shape the lives of individuals. As in *Fools of Fortune*, the history that Trevor is concerned with in *The Silence in the Garden* is one of violence and division, one in which the humanistic principles of compassion and connection have been edged offstage by political and religious fanaticism. And so the novel has a tragic shape, with history providing the necessary tragic inevitability. Indeed, it is a more faithfully, more relentlessly tragic novel than is *Fools of Fortune*; no hint of redemption is allowed to surface at the end of the book, only evidence of loss and decay, of the promise of the future destroyed by the sins of the past.

In matters of style and structure, *The Silence in the Garden* is closer to Trevor's English novels than it is to *Fools of Fortune*. The first-person point of view used in the earlier Irish book is discarded for the more characteristic third-person point of view that moves between a distanced, neutral narrative voice and voices heavily influenced by certain characters. The novel also is structured around multiple centers of consciousness, and employs a relatively large cast of characters drawn from a broad range of social classes. Finally, it uses the device of a character who takes on the role of truth-teller, a would-be agent of moral reform or moral responsibility.

The novel is set for the most part in 1931, but the first chapter collapses the years between 1904 and 1931 into a series of brief vignettes recorded in the diaries of a poor relation of the Rolleston family named Sarah Pollexfen (the Yeatsian echo surely is deliberate). This structure forces the reader to view the present and speculate on the future through the lens of the past, and the present and the future of the Rolleston family are determined in large part by the events that took place betwen 1904 and 1931, including the central event of the novel, the murder of the family's butler by the IRA during the Anglo-Irish War. Moreover, because the events during these troubled years are only hinted at in the first chapter, the reader is encouraged continually to reconstruct that past as more and more fragments of it become available in the course of the novel, and so is constantly made aware of the present as shaped by the past.

The use of multiple centers of consciousness has a similar effect, forcing the reader to see the present in terms of various subjective impressions that are, in different ways, products of the past. Most of the characters who function as centers of consciousness have been damaged in one way or another by Ireland's history of violence and division. The lives of the three Rolleston children all are stunted, for reasons that only gradually become clear: John James, the oldest, was wounded in the First World War not long after his father died at Passchendaele, and is now reduced to a life of inertia relieved only by a sordid liaison with a plump, simpering widow who runs a local boarding-house called, of all things, the Rose of Tralee; Lionel, the second son, also unmarried and childless, has withdrawn from family and society, and dedicated himself exclusively to the mundane task of running the farm; and Villana, the beautiful, brilliant daughter once pledged to marry Sarah's brother Hugh inexplicably decides to marry the stiff and pompous family solicitor, Finnamore Balt. There is also young Tom, the illegitimate child of the family's maid Brigid and the butler Linchy, a boy haunted by the feeling that he is marked by the sin of his parents, alienated from the community by the circumstances of his birth.

The novel's most important center of consciousness is Mrs Rolleston, the grandmother of the three Rolleston children (their mother died giving birth to Villana), and approaching 90 when Sarah Pollexfen returns to the family house, Carriglas, in 1931, after an absence of about a dozen years. Not only is Mrs Rolleston's memory a repository of the past, but also she is the one character in the novel who insists that history has moral consequences that must be faced, that the past cannot be forgotten or repressed. In a long conversation with Sarah that takes place near the end of the novel and is recorded in Sarah's diaries, Mrs Rolleston emerges in the role of truth-teller, an authorial figure of sorts, with Sarah as her amanuensis, committed to setting the record straight even if it might not make any difference: "She said she wanted it written down. She wanted it in Sarah Pollexfen's diaries, so that the truth could be passed on. Or left behind, whichever way you looked at it."[22]

It is through Mrs Rolleston's memory that most of the dark secrets of the Rolleston family gradually surface – especially the incident in which, when Sarah was first at Carriglas as governess, the children, including Sarah's brother Hugh, hunted and tortured a young Catholic boy on the island, at one point even threatening him with a gun. It is through Mrs Rolleston's memory that the connection is drawn between this event and the murder of Linchy in 1920. Linchy was, in fact, killed accidentally; the explosives that blew him to pieces were intended for the Rolleston children, and they were placed in the avenue leading to the house at Carriglas by Cornelius Dowley, the boy they once tortured and now a prominent figure in the IRA. And it is through Mrs Rolleston's memory that the consequences of Dowley's act are revealed, how he was hunted down and, this time, shot by the Black-and-Tans on the doorstep of a local billiard-hall, and how his mother committed suicide by walking into the sea. It is all, Mrs Rolleston tells Sarah, part of *"a thread of carnage that was unbearable even to think about"* (p. 186) – a thread, moreover, made specifically from the prejudices and divisions embedded in Ireland's historical consciousness. As Mrs Rolleston also says to Sarah of her grandchildren, *"In another place and another time they would have grown up healthily to exorcise their aberrations by shrugging them away"* (p. 187).

The impossibility of doing that, at least in Ireland, is dramatized partly in the way that past events keep intruding – in brief, usually involuntary flashes – into Mrs Rolleston's consciousness. The following passage, for example, shifts rapidly between a subjective description of Mrs Rolleston's bedroom to a sudden memory of the night that Linchy was killed, then to a memory of a letter written by another maid at Carriglas, a young girl who was, at the time, supposedly in love with Cornelius Dowley and who was sent away by the family, and finally to a general reflection about the moral force of past actions:

A fire burned in the bedroom, as it always did during the winter months. The lamp on the dressing-table cast a soft, yellow light. For more than seventy years she had slept in this room. The son she had outlived had been conceived and born here. Her tears had dampened the yielding warmth of the bed she lay down in now, tears of pleasure often. 'I'm so sorry, Brigid,' she tried to comfort when Brigid had wept also. 'I'm so very sorry.' The remains had lain with a sheet drawn over them, one sheet replaced by another because the blood still oozed. *Mightn't it appease the conscience if you sent a few shillings?* But conscience stayed to mock, and to insist upon as its greater due.

(p. 182)

Part of the record that Mrs Rolleston wants to bring out into the open is embedded in the island of Carriglas itself. Like so many places in Ireland, this island off the coast of Co. Cork (the name of which comes from the Irish "carraig glas," or green rock, referring to an optical illusion[23]) is layered with fragments from history, much of it violent and divisive. There are standing stones on the island, huge burial markers that are also remnants of the warring pre-Christian civilizations that once inhabited Ireland. The island also contains the ruins of an abbey, a relic from Ireland's medieval Christian period and so a reminder of the ancient conflict between pagan and Christian. The Rolleston house is steeped in a past of usurpation and violence; it was built not long after the first Rollestons, arriving in Ireland in the wake of Cromwell's bloody conquest of the seventeenth century, had driven another family off the island and sent them, as Finnamore Balt says, "on their way to the stony wilderness of Mayo" (p. 41). There is also much uncultivated land on the island, a sign of the catastrophic Great Famine in the 1840s. Finally, the bridge to the mainland that is being built in 1931 suggests both that the insularity of life on Carriglas can no longer be supported in the new Ireland of the twentieth century, and, since the town has decided to dedicate the bridge to Cornelius Dowley, that the Rollestons' status in the community is no longer what it once was.

The precipitous decline of Carriglas in the years between Sarah's first visit there in 1908, when she arrived to be governess, and her return in 1931 is also marked by the destruction and corruption of love, a theme that is central to much of Trevor's writing. The love of Villana and Hugh is poisoned by their past acts of cruelty to Cornelius Dowley, and by the consequences that have sprung, with tragic inevitability, from them. Again, it is Mrs Rolleston who, in her final talk with Sarah, insists on recognizing the moral implications of past actions:

Your brother and Villana turned away from all they felt for one another, and perhaps they had to. For how could their children play in that same garden and not ever be told of what had festered so horribly in a wound? How could the reason for the tragedy on the avenue not ever be revealed? Was it to be kept from them that the cornering of Cornelius Dowley on the steps of a billiard-hall was an irony and a repetition? Was it to be kept from them that his mother walked out into the waves? And that all

159

of it began in the idyll of a lazy summer?

(p. 187)

Villana's marriage to Finnamore Balt is a crippled, reductive version of her love for Hugh; for Villana, the marriage is motivated by a desire to repress her memories of Hugh, and for Finnamore, nineteen years her elder, it is an arrangement based at least as much on professional grounds – he now can more easily bring to fruition, he thinks, his solicitor's dream of restoring the land of the Rolleston estate to what it was before the Great Famine – as on feeling or passion. This motif of frustrated or failed love is also reflected in Sarah's unrequited yearnings for Lionel, and, in another way, in John James's tawdry affair with Mrs Moledy, the mistress of the Rose of Tralee.

Not surprisingly, the Rolleston children leave no heirs (one of the conditions of Villana's marriage to Finnamore Balt is that there be no children), and so, after the death of Sarah in 1971, Carriglas falls, ironically, to Tom, not only a Catholic, but also the illegitimate son of a family maid and the family butler. It is Tom's consciousness that, in the last chapter of the novel, set in 1971, bears witness to the end of the Rolleston family, but Tom is an important character in other ways. His experiences as a young boy growing up on Carriglas and in the mainland town are related to a theme common to much twentieth-century Irish writing – the conflict between individual values and freedom and the repressive, puritanical attitudes frequently associated with Irish Catholicism. Some of Tom's feelings of alienation are generated by nuns at the convent school he attends, some by local towns-people, and some by the perversely religious Holy Mullihan, a boy a few years older than Tom who dogs him with stories designed to feed his guilt. "It's like you'd walk up to the Cross and spit on our Lord," he tells Tom at one point. "When your mother committed the sin, Tom, another thorn was established in the crown" (p. 87). Although it is not surprising to learn that Holy Mullihan has his crooked heart set on becoming a priest, Tom's guilt has at least as much to do with Trevor's concern with the burden of the past as it does with conventional anti-Catholicism in Ireland. Tom is living very much in the shadow of a past over which he has no control, and one decidedly colored by the political and religious violence that has so insidiously engulfed Carriglas;

Linchy and Brigid were planning to marry, and so had it not been for the IRA explosives, intended for the Rolleston children, Tom's life would, presumably, have been very different.

Although Tom's life is, in fact, tragically determined, as are the lives of most of the characters in the novel, *The Silence in the Garden* contains its fair share of the closely and ironically observed comedy of manners that has become a trademark of Trevor's writing. The premier comic scene in the novel – and it is one of the best in all of Trevor's fiction – is that in which Mrs Moledy shows up, drunk and uninvited, at Villana's wedding lunch on the lawn at Carriglas. Much of the comedy in the scene derives, characteristically, from confusion and from the gap between intention and action; Mrs Moledy's plan to hide behind the trees surrounding the lawn before the lunch guests arrive, and so get John James's attention without anyone knowing she is there, is foiled when she finds herself seated at the head of the table as the guests are arriving, and unable, because of all that she has drunk, to get up. The result is vintage Trevor, especially in the way that the comedy in the dialogue is played off against Mrs Moledy's perceptions and misperceptions (she is the center of consciousness throughout the scene), which tend to generate some sympathy for her even at her worst moment:

'I need to get into the trees,' Mrs Moledy said to the Bishop of Killaloe. 'I shouldn't be loitering here.'
'Trees?'
'I'm here on business, as a matter of fact.'
The glass she'd filled to the brim was still on the table in front of her. She lifted it to her lips and found that the whiskey it contained had been pleasantly warmed by the sun. She remarked upon this to the Bishop, adding that she always preferred the addition of a drop of warm water, although she hadn't asked for it, not being in a public house. 'Haven't they a lovely place here, though?' she said, endeavouring to be friendly.
Other people were beginning to sit down. She waved at a man from the Bank of Ireland, whom she knew to talk to, and at Miss de Ryal, whom she knew by sight. The Commodium female was there, extraordinary that they'd invite the like of that.

'Well, isn't this great?' she remarked to the Bishop.

'Isn't what great?'

'Errah, go on with you!' She nudged his elbow with her own. As soon as she'd finished the contents of her glass she'd slip away, no trouble to anyone. At the far end of the table, where the old grandmother was being assisted on to a chair, the sister was directing people to other chairs. He was standing just behind her, directing people also. She waved at him when he was looking straight at her, but he took no notice.

(p. 151)

This scene provides more than comic relief. The political and religious divisions that have poisoned life at Carriglas, and in fact led to this very wedding, are visible here, but in a comic mode. Indeed, the very thing upon which the comedy in this scene chiefly depends – the inappropriateness of Mrs Moledy's presence at such a social gathering – points to a set of attitudes that, in other circumstances, produce results decidedly more tragic than comic.

Those attitudes are rooted in a history of political and religious differences that are, regrettably, visible still. *The Silence in the Garden* has little to do directly with the sectarian violence in contemporary Northern Ireland, but it has much to say indirectly about what lies behind that violence, and about what makes the issues being fought over so difficult to resolve. In the scene in which Mrs Rolleston unburdens herself of what she knows about Carriglas and the dark secrets of its past, Sarah tries at one point to stop her, using the well-worn argument that all these events should be forgotten because they "belong to the past." Mrs Rolleston's response embodies much of the wisdom of this novel, and suggests at the same time that its characters and events, precisely because they are set in the past, have a genuinely important bearing on today's troubled present. "*The past has no belongings,*" Mrs Rolleston says. "*The past does not obligingly absorb what is not wanted*" (p. 185).

What is not wanted, presumably, is what Yeats had in mind in writing these oft-quoted lines:

> Out of Ireland have we come.
> Great hatred, little room,
> Maimed us at the start.
> I carry from my mother's womb
> A fanatic heart.[24]

162

It should be remembered, moreover, that Yeats was almost always writing out of a vision that transcended Ireland, and the same might be said for William Trevor. After all, Attracta and Cynthia, Willie and Marianne, Villana and Mrs Rolleston hardly stand alone among Trevor's characters as victims of fanaticism. From the eccentric Mr Jaraby to the calculating Francis Tyte, from the lonely Mr Jeffs to the naive Miss Simpson, almost all of Trevor's characters live in worlds in which fanaticism of one sort or another holds sway. It may be less visible or less violent than the views expressed in podium and pulpit in contemporary Ulster, but it is fanaticism none the less – the subtle, destructive fanaticism of the alienated and the lost. In writing about his native Ireland, Trevor is, in fact, writing as well about what concerns him most, and what gives his work much of its force and significance for readers Irish and non-Irish alike: the lonely, fanatic heart of contemporary man.

NOTES

1 "ONLY CONNECT": *Introduction*

1 *The Complete Poems and Plays* (New York: Harcourt, Brace & World, 1934, 1935, 1936, 1952), p. 46.

2 Trevor's eleven novels are: *A Standard of Behaviour* (London: Hutchinson, 1958); *The Old Boys* (London: Bodley Head, 1964); *The Boarding-House* (London: Bodley Head, 1965); *The Love Department* (London: Bodley Head, 1966); *Mrs Eckdorf in O'Neill's Hotel* (London: Bodley Head, 1969); *Miss Gomez and the Brethren* (London: Bodley Head, 1971); *Elizabeth Alone* (London: Bodley Head, 1973); *The Children of Dynmouth* (London: Bodley Head, 1976); *Other People's Worlds* (London: Bodley Head, 1980); *Fools of Fortune* (London: Bodley Head, 1983); and *The Silence in the Garden* (London: Bodley Head, 1988). His six collections of short stories are: *The Day We Got Drunk on Cake and Other Stories* (London: Bodley Head, 1967); *The Ballroom of Romance and Other Stories* (London: Bodley Head, 1972); *Angels at the Ritz and Other Stories* (London: Bodley Head, 1975); *Lovers of Their Time and Other Stories* (London: Bodley Head, 1978); *Beyond the Pale and Other Stories* (London: Bodley Head, 1981); and *The News from Ireland and Other Stories* (London: Bodley Head, 1986). Trevor has also published a novella, *Nights at the Alexandra* (New York: Harper & Row, 1987); a book about Irish writing and landscape, *A Writer's Ireland: Landscape in Literature* (New York: Viking, 1984); and a collection of stories and memoirs, *Old School Ties* (London: Lemon Tree Press, 1976). In addition, the stories in his first five volumes were published as *The Stories of William Trevor* (New York: Penguin, 1983), and a selection of Irish stories was published as *The Distant Past* (Dublin: Poolbeg Press, 1979). Trevor has also written numerous radio plays and television scripts based on his short stories. He has published two full-length plays: *The Old Boys* (London: Davis Poynter, 1971) and *Scenes from an Album* (Dublin: Co-Op Books, 1981). He has also published the following one-act plays: *The Girl* (London: Samuel French, 1968); *Going Home* (London: Samuel French, 1972); *A Night with Mrs da Tanka* (London: Samuel French, 1972); *Marriages* (London: Samuel French, 1974); and *A Perfect*

Relationship (London: Burnham House, 1976).

3 Aside from reviews and interviews, the critical work on Trevor consists of the following essays: Mark Mortimer, "William Trevor in Dublin," *Etudes Irlandaises*, 4 (1975), pp. 77–85; Julian Gitzen, "The Truth-Tellers of William Trevor," *Critique: Studies in Modern Fiction*, 21, No. 1 (1979), pp. 59–72; Jay L. Halio and Paul Binding, "William Trevor," *Dictionary of Literary Biography, Vol. 14: British Novelists Since 1960* (Detroit: Gale Press, 1983), pp. 723–30; Robert E. Rhodes, "William Trevor's Stories of the Troubles," in James D. Brophy and Raymond J. Porter (eds) *Contemporary Irish Writing* (Boston: Iona College Press, 1983), pp. 95–114; Mark Mortimer, "The Short Stories of William Trevor," *Etudes Irlandaises*, 9 (1984), pp. 161–73; John J. Stinson, "Replicas, Foils, and Revelation in Some 'Irish' Short Stories of William Trevor," *The Canadian Journal of Irish Studies*, 11, No. 2 (1985), pp. 17–26. Trevor's short stories are also discussed in Robert Hogan, "Old Bucks, Young Bucks, and New Women: The Contemporary Irish Short Story," in James F. Kilroy ed. *The Irish Short Story: A Critical History* (Boston: Twayne, 1984), pp. 182–6.

4 "William Trevor," in Peter Firchow ed. *The Writer's Place: Interviews on the Literary Situation in Contemporary Britain* (Minneapolis: University of Minnesota Press, 1974), p. 306.

5 "William Trevor," interview by Mark Ralph-Bowman, *The Transatlantic Review*, No. 53/54 (1976), p. 7.

6 "Between Holyhead and Dun Laoghaire," review of *The Collected Stories of Elizabeth Bowen*, *The Times Literary Supplement*, (6 Feb. 1981), p. 131.

7 "The Old Boy," interview with Trevor by Sean Dunne, *The Sunday Tribune*, (Dublin), (2 June 1985), p. 17.

8 *Old School Ties* (London: Lemon Tree Press, 1976), p. 18.

9 The relationship between Trevor's work as a sculptor and his writing, particularly his interest in the formal aspects of short stories and novels, has been described by Trevor himself: "Being a sculptor does help you to form things. There's a way in which you think as a sculptor. You see things in the round very much. You have to have an extra something; you have to go see around the back of somebody's head, as it were. And I've found that I still think like that when I'm writing. I'm still obsessed by form and pattern – the actual shape of things, the shape of a novel or the shape of a short story" (Amanda Smith, "*PW* Interviews William Trevor," *Publishers Weekly*, (28 Oct. 1983), p. 80).

10 "Distiller of the Extraordinary," interview-article by Nicholas Shakespeare, *The Times*, (15 March 1986), p. 23.

11 In "Distiller of the Extraordinary," interview-article by Nicholas Shakespeare, *The Times*, (15 March 1986), Trevor is quoted as saying about marriage: "It is the closest of all relationships because people choose. They dig their own graves. I don't write about happy marriage because I don't think you can analyse happiness" (p. 23).

12 Quoted, from an article in *London Magazine*, in *Contemporary Authors*, vols. 9–12 (Detroit: Gale Research, 1974), p. 193.

13 Quoted in Denis Donoghue, review of *Field Work*, *New York Times Book Review*, (2 Dec. 1979), p. 46.

14 *The Silence in the Garden* (London: Bodley Head, 1988), p. 186.

15 "William Trevor," interview by Mark Ralph-Bowman, *The Transatlantic Review*, No. 53/54 (1976), p. 12. Trevor also said, in the same interview: "You let them [readers] down if you can't present them with some kind of coherent story that works. It is a business of communication. . . . That is a personal statement because I don't like abstract novels any more than I like abstract art" (p. 6). And when asked to identify writers that he admired, he listed Charles Dickens, George Eliot, Jane Austen, Mrs Gaskell, Thomas Hardy, E. M. Forster, and P. G. Wodehouse (pp. 7–8).

16 Robert Scholes and Robert Kellogg, in *The Nature of Narrative* (New York: Oxford University Press, 1966), have argued that for the modern reader the only credible narrator is, paradoxically, one who is suspect: "A narrator who is not in some way suspect, who is not in some way subject to ironic scrutiny is what the modern temper finds least bearable" (p. 277). Trevor's distrust of narrative omniscience clearly places him in this tradition, which is based on a philosophical relativism or scepticism. As Scholes and Kellogg say, the ironic gap that is exploited in modern fiction is between "limited understanding which is real, and an ideal of absolute truth which is itself suspect" (p. 277).

17 Patrick Swinden, *The English Novel of History and Society, 1940–1980* (New York: St Martin's Press, 1984), p. 12.

18 *Beyond the Pale and Other Stories* (London: Bodley Head, 1981), p. 108.

2   "A FARCE IN A VALE OF TEARS": *The Early Novels*

1 *A Standard of Behaviour* (London: Hutchinson, 1958; reprinted London: Sphere Books, 1982), p. 1. All quotations are from this edition.

2 *The Old Boys* (London: Bodley Head, 1964), pp. 7–8. All quotations are from this edition.

3 Among reviews of *The Old Boys* are "Hanged by a School-Tie," *The Times Literary Supplement*, (5 March 1964), p. 189, and J. D. Scott, "School Days That Never Ended," *New York Times Book Review*, (29 March 1964), p. 26; of *The Boarding-House*, "Castle Heartrent," *The Times Literary Supplement*, (6 May 1965), p. 345, and Victor Chapin, "Rooms for Misfits," *Saturday Review*, (26 June 1965), p. 39; of *The Love Department*, "Under Restraint," *The Times Literary Supplement*, (22 Sept. 1966), p. 873, Martin Levin, untitled review, *New York Times Book Review*, (15 Jan. 1967), p. 44, and Lawrence Graver, "Daftness Falls from the Air," *The New Republic*, (4 Feb. 1967), pp. 35–7.

4 *The Love Department* (London: Bodley Head, 1966), p. 294. All quotations are from this edition.

5   More commonly, Ivy Compton-Burnett is cited as influencing Trevor's dialogue. See, for example, Jay L. Halio and Paul Binding, "William Trevor," in *Dictionary of Literary Biography, Vol. 14: British Novelists Since 1960* (Detroit: Gale Research, 1983), pp. 723–30. Trevor himself has acknowledged a debt to Compton-Burnett, saying that "she writes in a very old-fashioned style and I write in an old-fashioned style" ("William Trevor," interviewed by Mark Ralph-Bowman, *The Transatlantic Review*, No. 53/54 (1976), p. 11).

6   See, for example, "Hanged by a School-Tie," *The Times Literary Supplement*, (5 March 1964), p. 189.

7   In the review entitled "Castle Heartrent," *The Times Literary Supplement*, (6 May 1965), the anonymous reviewer said: "Details are provided but every event and remark seem more angular than life. His characters carry their eccentricities like large labels" (p. 345).

8   "William Trevor," interview by Mark Ralph-Bowman, *The Transatlantic Review*, No. 53/54 (1976), pp. 9–10.

9   *The Boarding-House* (London: Bodley Head, 1965), pp. 283–4, 286. All quotations are from this edition.

10 See Julian Gitzen, "The Truth-Tellers of William Trevor," *Critique: Studies in Modern Fiction*, 21, No. 1 (1979), pp. 65–6, for a discussion of Mr Bird's character along these lines.

11 Chapter Twelve, for example, is devoted entirely to what is essentially a piece of slapstick – the mix-up over Mr Bird's clothing. Also, the lengthy discussion in the boarding-house lounge that takes up most of the preceding chapter, and that includes a good deal of talk about trained birds and trained fish, does very little to advance either plot or characterization.

12 The same obsession with her wedding-day is used, as noted earlier, to develop the relatively minor character of Janice Rush in *The Boarding-House*. It is also used later for Julia Ferndale in *Other People's Worlds*.

13 The same technique is used, with similar effect, in an early scene in *The Boarding-House* describing the burial of Mr Bird. The center of consciousness in this scene moves in and out of several of the residents standing around the grave, but near the end of the scene, another character is introduced, a woman visiting the grave of a relative, solely to provide a slightly distanced perspective on the residents:

> A visitor to the graveyard, renewing wall-flowers in a jam-pot above a relative's remains, glanced up from her task and saw across the headstones and the crosses this little knot of assorted people, one very tall and one black, being harangued apparently by a small man. The lady hastened with the flowers, for she found it at once intriguing that such a scene should be enacted in a graveyard.

> (p. 25)

14 A different criticism of the book, one that assumes little depth of

NOTES

characterization, is made by Lawrence Graver, "Daftness Falls from the Air", *The New Republic*, (4 Feb. 1967): "Trevor throughout has been so poised, so careful to refine the dryness of the farce and to screen the characters from complex emotions, that he seems finally to be toying with the large subjects on which the book so obviously rests. In the earlier novels, the fastidious style matched the modesty of the subject-matter; now the crowded canvas and the tools of the miniaturist are incompatible" (p. 37).

3 "THE ODOUR OF THE ASHPITS": *The Middle Novels*

1 "William Trevor," interview by Mark Ralph-Bowman, *The Transatlantic Review*, No. 53/54 (1976), p. 8.

2 "William Trevor," in Peter Firchow ed. *The Writer's Place: Interviews on the Literary Situation in Contemporary Britain* (Minneapolis: University of Minnesota Press, 1974), p. 306. The argument for reading *Mrs Eckdorf in O'Neill's Hotel* as an Irish novel has been made, largely on the grounds of the accuracy with which Trevor describes Dublin and its inhabitants, by Mark Mortimer, "William Trevor in Dublin," *Etudes Irlandaises*, 4 (1975), pp. 77–85.

3 Martin Levin, review of *Mrs Eckdorf in O'Neill's Hotel*, New York Times Book Review, (15 June 1970), says that the stage-setting for the novel "would seem at home in Joyce's *Dubliners*, as would the frustrated souls who frequent the hotel of the title" (p. 43).

4 Mrs Sinnott bears some striking resemblance to Mr Bird of *The Boarding-House*: both are old, Mr Bird dying at the beginning of *The Boarding-House* and Mrs Sinnott at the end of *Mrs Eckdorf in O'Neill's Hotel*; both try, and fail, to create communities by taking in social outcasts and misfits; both function somewhat as author-surrogates, Mr Bird in his "Notes on Residents" and in his role as creator of the boarding-house (as opposed to the creator of *The Boarding-House*), and Mrs Sinnott, less actively, in her red exercise-books, which constitute another version of many of the events in the novel. See also Julian Gitzen, "The Truth-Tellers of William Trevor," *Critique: Studies in Modern Fiction*, 21, No. 1 (1979), pp. 68–9.

5 *Mrs Eckdorf in O'Neill's Hotel* (London: Bodley Head, 1969), pp. 17–18. All quotations are from this edition.

6 *Miss Gomez and the Brethren* (London: Bodley Head, 1971), p. 37. All quotations are from this edition.

7 Jonathan Raban, "Crow Street," review of *Miss Gomez and the Brethren*, New Statesman, (15 Oct. 1971), makes a similar argument: "Mr Trevor has always been a master of fey, priggish verbal comedy. But in *Miss Gomez and the Brethren* he has created a full and dark landscape of abandonment; and he has learned to show the bewilderment and despair that lurks in the wide spaces separating word from word in his fustily elegant grammar" (p. 514).

8 Julian Gitzen, "The Truth-Tellers of William Trevor," *Critique:*

168

Studies in Modern Fiction, 21, No. 1 (1979), p. 70.

9 This argument is advanced in an anonymous review of *Miss Gomez and the Brethren*, "Progress against Loneliness," *The Times Literary Supplement*, (15 Oct. 1971): "The emptiness of Miss Gomez's philosophy before her conversion is tacitly accepted by the author; and subsequently it is the religious Miss Gomez who is discredited, not that early emptiness" (p. 1247).

10 "William Trevor," interview by Mark Ralph-Bowman, *The Transatlantic Review*, No. 53/54 (1976), p. 10.

11 Jonathan Raban, "Crow Street," *New Statesman*, (15 Oct. 1971), makes this argument: "Mr Trevor's style achieves its force by a deliberate narrowing of social tone; it registers, with a wonderful formal accuracy, a stunned disbelief before the sheer muddle and violence of the world it catalogues so carefully. It is the language of the lost and abandoned as they vainly try to match their impoverished repertoire of words to the appalling scope of their experience" (p. 514).

12 *Elizabeth Alone* (London: Bodley Head, 1973), p. 9. All quotations are from this edition.

13 Martin Levin, review of *Elizabeth Alone*, *New York Times Book Review*, (30 June 1974), argues that the book reveals "four styles of hopelessness," and that they are unified by the perception of Miss Samson: "The point of it all is clear only to a mad visionary like Miss Samson" (p. 31).

14 This argument is advanced in an anonymous review of *Elizabeth Alone*, "The Flavour of Failure," *The Times Literary Supplement*, (26 Oct. 1973): "The end of *Elizabeth Alone* suggests a tentative answer to a self-posed question: What is all this human ridiculousness ultimately about? . . . Mr Trevor's answer is that it is about the possibility of compassion" (p. 1299). Referring specifically to the final scene between Elizabeth and Miss Samson, the reviewer says: "This is a comparatively unspectacular sort of affirmation; but any kind of affirmation at all is difficult for a writer of novels like Mr Trevor's to bring off" (p. 1299).

15 Anon., "The Flavour of Failure", *The Times Literary Supplement*, (26 Oct. 1973): "Henry is one of Mr Trevor's most triumphant comic inventions, a piercingly credible failure whose life trundles rapidly downhill despite all his efforts to save it" (p. 1299).

16 Letter to Grant Richards, 23 June 1906, quoted in Richard Ellman ed., *Selected Letters of James Joyce* (New York: Viking, 1957, 1966, 1975), p. 89.

17 James Joyce, *Ulysses* (1922; reprinted Vintage Books, 1961), p. 333.

4 "OTHER PEOPLE'S PAIN": *The Late Novels*

1 "William Trevor," interview by Mark Ralph-Bowman, *The Transatlantic Review*, No. 53/54 (1976), p. 7.

2 *The Children of Dynmouth* (London: Bodley Head, 1976), pp. 115–16. All quotations are from this edition.

3 A number of critics have, none the less, read the book in this way, and then condemned Trevor for ending the novel with a cheap brand of optimism. Russell Davies, in "Tiny Tim," review of *The Children of Dynmouth*, *New Statesman*, (9 July 1976), says: "Whatever the social likelihoods of Timothy's case might be, he has been brought to a pitch of literary malice which can't simply be allowed to fall away like this. . . . He [Trevor] is guilty of failing to respect the impetus generated by his own characterisation, and of reasserting the decencies of life in a way that the whole tendency of the story belies, negates and derides" (p. 53). Duncan Fallowell, in "Time-wasting," review of *The Children of Dynmouth*, *Spectator*, (19 June 1976), suggests that the book would have been better had Timothy been allowed to put on his one-man routine; instead, Fallowell argues, "the book is finished with finger-pointing and silly recriminations while Lavinia Featherston, the vicar's wife who hasn't done anything up to now except clean jam off the kitchen window, gets a glimpse of how God moves in mysterious ways and sees in Timothy a chance to compensate on her miscarriage" (p. 25). And Anne Duchéne, in "The Decencies Observed," review of *The Children of Dynmouth*, *The Times Literary Supplement*, (18 June 1976), compares the book to earlier Trevor novels, concluding: "What is surprising in this book is an appreciable extension in the area of pity, which at the end seems also somewhat to unsettle Mr Trevor's customary elegance" (p. 731). A reading more sensitive to Trevor's characteristic, qualifying irony at the end of the novel is provided by Joyce Carol Oates, in "More Lovely than Evil," review of *The Children of Dynmouth*, *New York Times Book Review*, (17 April 1977): "And so there is the possibility of redemption; or if not redemption, at least a place in the community. But it is all very tenuous, very problematic. The novel ends abruptly and ironically, and nothing is really resolved" (p. 36).

4 In writing in her diary about the process of composing *Mrs Dalloway*, Woolf said: "I should say a good deal about *The Hours* [an earlier title for *Mrs Dalloway*] and my discovery: how I dig out beautiful caves behind my characters: I think that gives exactly what I want; humanity, humour, depth. The idea is that the caves shall connect and each comes to daylight at the present moment" (quoted in Virginia Woolf, *A Writer's Diary* (New York: Harcourt Brace Jovanovich, 1953), p. 59). Trevor uses a technique something like this in earlier novels – most notably, perhaps, in *Elizabeth Alone* – but not as efficiently as he does in his two late novels. Also, the idea of invisible or underground connections existing between various characters is appropriate to Trevor's thematic concerns as well as to his formal techniques.

NOTES

5   From "Apology," a preface to *Late Lyrics and Earlier* (1922); quoted in Donald Davie, *Thomas Hardy and British Poetry* (New York: Oxford University Press, 1972), p. 7.

6   Again, this method of characterization is very close to that described by Virginia Woolf in her diary entry about *Mrs Dalloway*. Moreover, the character of Julia Ferndale – even apart from her relish for parties – would seem to owe more than a little to that of Clarissa Dalloway.

7   *Other People's Worlds* (London: Bodley Head, 1980), p. 28. All quotations are from this edition.

8   Frank Tuohy, in "Seeing How the Other Half Lives," review of *Other People's Worlds*, *The Times Literary Supplement*, (20 June 1980), argues, rather narrowly, that none of Trevor's working-class characters in the novel, with the possible exception of Joy, has any redeeming features. "They represent sloth, menace and ultimate destruction," he says. He also describes Trevor as "the latest in a line of Anglo-Irish writers who have seen Irish, and then English, life as involving a caste system, rather than as a multitude of social classes where boundaries are always breaking down" (p. 690). Trevor's treatment of the lower classes is also discussed in John Updike, review of *Other People's Worlds*, *The New Yorker*, (23 March 1981), pp. 154–7.

9   For a less than sympathetic, single-minded reading of Francis's character, see Jack Beatty, "Hell in Other People," review of *Other People's Worlds*, *The New Republic*, (7 Feb. 1981): ". . . the most unsuitable thing about Francis is that he is evil, even Evil" (p. 38).

10 For a discussion of Julia's character and its thematic significance, see Benjamin DeMott, "No Woman Is an Island," review of *Other People's Worlds*, *New York Times Book Review*, (1 Feb. 1981), pp. 8, 19; and Penelope Lively, "Lifescapes," review of *Other People's Worlds* and others, *Encounter*, 55, No. 5 (Nov. 1980), p. 63.

11 John Lucas, in a review of *Other People's Worlds* and *The Boarding-House* (a reissue), *New Statesman*, (4 July 1980), says of Francis: "He has endless imagination but no imaginativeness" (p. 23).

5   "SUCH TALES OF WOE": *The Short Stories*

1   Victoria Glendinning in a review of *Lovers of Their Time*, "Oblique Approaches to Major Passions," *New York Times Book Review*, (8 April 1979), makes much the same point about Trevor as a short-story writer: "His oblique approach to large passions and his faithful rendering of the texture of domestic life make him a miniaturist" (p. 26). And in a review of *The Children of Dynmouth*, "The Decencies Observed," *The Times Literary Supplement*, (18 June 1976), Anne Duchêne says of Trevor: ". . . the territory of unease, the sure-footed sinister prowl round the edges of pain, at which he excels, is less easily handled in a novel than in short stories, where he need only strike a disquieting chord and leave it to vibrate in the reader's mind" (p. 731).

171

NOTES

2 See Clare Hanson, *Short Stories and Short Fictions, 1880–1980* (New York: St Martin's Press, 1985), pp. 112–39, for a full treatment of the free story.

3 Walter Allen, *The Short Story in English* (New York: Oxford University Press, 1981), says of Joyce: "Joyce's great achievement in *Dubliners* is to have replaced the anecdotal basis of the story with a structure of symbolism" (p. 115).

4 V. S. Pritchett, in a review of *Lovers of Their Time*, "Explosion of Conscience," *The New York Review of Books*, (19 April 1979), links Trevor to Chekhov and, by implication, the free story: "As his master Chekhov did, William Trevor simply, patiently, truthfully allows life to present itself, without preaching; he is the master of the small movements of conscience that worry away at the human imagination and our passions" (p. 8). Paul Theroux, in a review of *The Ballroom of Romance*, "Miseries and Splendours of the Short Story," *Encounter*, 39, No. 3 (1972), describes Trevor's style in his short stories as "spare and filled with suggestion" (p. 70). And David Harsent, reviewing *Angels at the Ritz*, "Tiny Tears," *New Statesman*, (24 Oct. 1975), says of Trevor's stories: ". . . the small quotidian horrors that afflict us and make us, finally, unknowable – the recollections, the gaucheries, the betrayals – float to the apparently placid surface of Trevor's prose without any frenzied stirring and lie there, unignorable" (p. 519).

5 Michael Gorra, "Laughter and Bloodshed," review of *Fools of Fortune*, *The Stories of William Trevor*, and other books, *The Hudson Review*, 37, No. 1 (1984), pp. 157–8, argues the comparison between Trevor and Carver.

6 Mary Gordon, in a review of *Fools of Fortune* and *The Stories of William Trevor* "The Luck of the Irish," *The New York Review of Books*, (22 Dec. 1983), calls Trevor "that highly realistic chronicler of the slow rot of English life" (p. 53), and Valentine Cunningham, in a review of *Angels at the Ritz*, "Sinking Fund," *The Times Literary Supplement*, (24 Oct. 1975), describes Trevor's characters as "Survivors, remnants, dregs – people and places and things clinging on against the odds, marooned relics of fuller lives, of past joys and once-glimpsed possibilities" (p. 1255). The argument can, however, be overstated, as it is by Robert Hogan, "Old Boys, Young Bucks, and New Women: The Contemporary Irish Short Story," in James F. Kilroy ed., *The Irish Short Story: A Critical History* (Boston: Twayne, 1984): ". . . in every aspect of life that Trevor has discussed – whether great or small, momentous or trivial – there is no respite from the seedy, the sordid, the disillusioning, the depressing, the ghastly, the horrible . . . in his low-keyed business-like fashion he quietly proceeds, story by story, to transform the entirety of modern life into a gray, dank, commonplace asylum" (p. 185).

7 "Sunday Drinks," in *Beyond the Pale and Other Stories* (London: Bodley Head, 1981), p. 240. All quotations are from this edition.

8 The comparison between Trevor and Updike is drawn by Robert

Towers in "Gleeful Misanthropy," review of *Fools of Fortune* and *The Stories of William Trevor*, *New York Times Book Review*, (2 Oct. 1983), p. 22.

9 *The Day We Got Drunk on Cake and Other Stories* (London: Bodley Head, 1967), pp. 112–13. All quotations are from this edition.

10 V.S. Pritchett, "Explosion of Conscience," *The New York Review of Books*, (19 April 1979), says of the characters in *Lovers of Their Time*: ". . . these people are not oddities but figures crucified by the continuity of evil and cruelty in human history, particularly the violent history of, say, the wars and cruelties of the last sixty years of this century" (p. 8). And Robert Towers, "Gleeful Misanthropy," *New York Times Book Review*, (2 Oct. 1983), says of Trevor's stories after the mid-1970s: "Violence, terrorism, melodrama – these are new elements in the work of a writer who had hitherto tended to subordinate the political to the personal" (p. 22).

11 This point is argued, surely too strenuously, by Peter Kemp, in a review of *Beyond the Pale*, "Cosiness and Carnage," *The Times Literary Supplement*, (16 Oct. 1981): ". . . he still mainly deals in types and caricatures. Only minimally individualized, they can't support the ponderous pronouncements about Evil he now loads upon them. . . . Ultimately, Trevor's small-scale world – two-dimensional and programmed to familiar routines – functions as a peep-show rather than a microcosm" (p. 1193).

12 Peter Buitenhuis, in a review of *The Day We Got Drunk on Cake*, "Prufrock Updated," *New York Times Book Review*, (11 Feb. 1968), says that this is the best story in the collection, and calls it "a fine study in the incongruity and absurdity of experience, written with extraordinary precision and controlled wit" (p. 38).

13 Frank O'Connor, *The Lonely Voice: A Study of the Short Story* (1962; 1963; London: Macmillan, 1965).

14 Trevor has also called attention to the connection between this story and *The Love Department*. In "William Trevor," interview by Mark Ralph-Bowman, *The Transatlantic Review*, No. 53/54 (1976), Trevor says: "I keep trying to get people like the Bolsovers (in *The Love Department*) right. . . . In 'Access to the Children,' the couple in the centre there were better than the Bolsovers. I think if I hadn't written about the Bolsovers I wouldn't have written that story" (pp. 5–6).

15 *The Ballroom of Romance and Other Stories* (London: Bodley Head, 1972), p. 7. All quotations are from this edition.

16 Paul Theroux, in "Miseries and Splendours of the Short Story," *Encounter*, 39, No. 3 (1972), says of *The Ballroom of Romance*: ". . . the thread that runs through all the stories is of brittle or urgent femininity thwarted by rather boorish maleness" (p. 70).

17 David Harsent, in "Tiny Tears," *New Statesman*, (24 Oct. 1975), says of this story: "Trevor effects a tension between youthful hopes recalled and the realities of middle-aged compromise; but he brings to that perfectly ordinary conflict a talent for invention and observation which reinvests it with an ineffable sadness" (p. 519).

18 *Angels at the Ritz and Other Stories* (London: Bodley Head, 1975), p. 65. All quotations are from this edition.

19 *Lovers of Their Time and Other Stories* (London: Bodley Head, 1978), pp. 17–18. All quotations are from this edition.

20 "The Tennis Court" was first published as a single story in *Angels at the Ritz*. It was reprinted in *Lovers of Their Time* as part of "Matilda's England."

21 *The News from Ireland and Other Stories* (London: Bodley Head, 1986), p. 69. All quotations are from this edition.

22 Bernard Bergonzi, "An Appendix on the Short Story," in *The Situation of the Novel* (Pittsburgh: University of Pittsburgh Press, 1970), has argued this point: "It seems to me that the modern short-story writer is bound to see the world in a certain way, not merely because of our customary atmosphere of crisis, but because the form of the short story tends to filter down experience to the prime elements of defeat and alienation" (p. 215). And Trevor himself has described the formal qualities of the modern short story in these terms: ". . . the short story of the 20th century has affinities with the Impressionists and the post-Impressionists. It is the art of the glimpse; it deals in echoes and reverberations; craftily it withholds information" ("Frank O'Connor: The Way of a Storyteller," review of *Collected Stories*, by Frank O'Connor, *Book World*, *The Washington Post*, (13 Sept. 1981), p. 1).

23 Frank O'Connor, *The Lonely Voice: A Study of the Short Story* (1962; 1963; London: Macmillan, 1965), p. 19.

24 "Sunday Drinks," in *Beyond the Pale and Other Stories* (London: Bodley Head, 1981), p. 241.

6 "THE WEIGHT OF CIRCUMSTANCES": *The Irish Fiction*

1 *Fools of Fortune* (London: Bodley Head, 1983), p. 160. All quotations are from this edition.

2 "The Ballroom of Romance," in *The Ballroom of Romance and Other Stories* (London: Bodley Head, 1972), p. 52. All quotations are from this edition.

3 Trevor has described modern Irish writing as a blend of these two distinct cultures, coming together, paradoxically enough, around the time of the division of Ireland into two separate nations, early in the twentieth century: "Yet even as that inept political division was born so, too, did the dream of cultural integration become a reality. The half-lost Ireland of the hedge-schools, of the oral tradition and the Irish language, crept into the warmth of Anglo-Irish hospitality" (*A Writer's Ireland: Landscape in Literature* (New York: Viking, 1984), p. 108).

4 "William Trevor," in Peter Firchow ed., *The Writer's Place: Interviews on the Literary Situation in Contemporary Britain* (Minneapolis: University of Minnesota Press, 1974), p. 306.

5 Trevor has argued for the advantages that this kind of cultural distance afforded earlier Anglo-Irish authors writing about Ireland: "It has been, even still is, popular to suggest that Somerville and Ross and Elizabeth Bowen were somehow not quite Irish, not properly or dedicatedly so. This view, while understandable, is a little glib. These three writers, because of a shared accident of birth saw the Ireland of William Carleton and later of Seumas O'Kelly from the same kind of distance as the one Joyce had to create for himself in order to dispel a certain claustrophobia" (*A Writer's Ireland: Landscape in Literature* (New York: Viking, 1984), p. 136).

6 John J. Stinson, "Replicas, Foils, and Revelation in Some 'Irish' Short Stories of William Trevor," *The Canadian Journal of Irish Studies*, 11, No. 2 (1985), has argued this point: "The essential loneliness of the human spirit and feelings of imprisonment of the human heart can be effectively shown when fictional characters are deftly placed within environments that are dull, stagnant, or oppressive. Ireland comes almost ready-made for the literary artist who wishes to reflect a primordial dilemma of the heart that lies too deep for ordinary words" (p. 19).

7 Stories in this category are "The Ballroom of Romance," "An Evening with John Joe Dempsey," and "A Choice of Butchers," from *The Ballroom of Romance*; "Teresa's Wedding" and "Mr McNamara," from *Angels at the Ritz*; "Death in Jerusalem" and "The Raising of Elvira Tremlett," from *Lovers of Their Time*; "The Paradise Lounge," from *Beyond the Pale*; "The Property of Colette Nervi," "Virgins," "Bodily Secrets," "Music," and "The Wedding in the Garden," from *The News from Ireland*.

8 Short stories in this category include "The Distant Past" in *Angels at the Ritz*; "Another Christmas," and "Attracta," in *Lovers of Their Time*; "Beyond the Pale" and "Autumn Sunshine," in *Beyond the Pale*; and "The News from Ireland," in *The News from Ireland*.

9 *Angels at the Ritz and Other Stories* (London: Bodley Head, 1975), p. 132. All quotations are from this edition.

10 John J. Stinson, "Replicas, Foils, and Revelation, in Some 'Irish' Short Stories of William Trevor," *The Canadian Journal of Irish Studies*, 11, No. 2 (1985), finds grounds for some optimism in the ending of this story: "Teresa's realization is a small one and a sad one, but, paradoxically, one that, at least in her mind, contains some hope. Teresa has had the benefit of the experience of her two older sisters; she sees her own life reflected in theirs and can learn from the reflection given back. She has also had pre-marital sexual experience, which her sisters have not. The story concludes on this note of slightly ambiguous hope after she has just admitted to her bridegroom that she once had a sexual encounter with one of his best friends" (p. 24).

11 *Beyond the Pale and Other Stories* (London: Bodley Head, 1981), pp. 254–5. All quotations are from this edition.

12 John J. Stinson, "Replicas, Foils, and Revelation in Some 'Irish'

Short Stories of William Trevor," *The Canadian Journal of Irish Studies*, 11, No. 2 (1985), says of the ending of this story: "No formal or technical element in the story is designed to incline the reader toward the acceptance of one or the other of these 'realizations.' Most readers will probably feel that the two do not really cancel each other out, but rather exist in a finely balanced counterpoise" (p. 22).

13 *The News from Ireland and Other Stories* (London: Bodley Head, 1986), p. 285. All quotations are from this edition.

14 *Nights at the Alexandra* (New York: Harper & Row, 1987), p. 11. All quotations are from this edition.

15 This narrative appeared in different form, under the title "Frau Messenger," in *The New Yorker*, (2 March 1987), pp. 30–9. In *The New Yorker* version, the story does not include the narrative frame so crucial to the development of Harry's character in the novella.

16 *A Writer's Ireland: Landscape in Literature* (New York: Viking, 1984), p. 51.

17 For a discussion of "The Distant Past," "Another Christmas," "Attracta," and "Autumn Sunshine," see Robert E. Rhodes, "William Trevor's Stories of the Troubles," in James D. Brophy and Raymond J. Porter, eds, *Contemporary Irish Writing* (Boston: Iona College Press, 1983), pp. 95–114. Rhodes argues that in these stories "the past not only represents itself but is a continuation of what for the Irish has been 'the cause that never dies' and for the protagonists results in almost every case in increased loneliness and isolation" (p. 98). Ann Hulbert, in a review of *Beyond the Pale*, *The New Republic*, (10 Feb. 1982), says of Trevor's Irish stories: "He also sketches in those pales that divide the daily delusions of personal lives from the horrors in the history of the two nations he knows from experience, Ireland and England" (p. 39). In a review of *Lovers of Their Time*, V. S. Pritchett says that Trevor's "art is to show they [his characters] have their part to play in an exceptional destiny, and even in a history beyond the private" ("Explosions of Conscience," *The New York Review of Books*, (19 April 1979), p. 8). Robert Towers, in "Good News," a review of *The News from Ireland*, *The New York Review of Books*, (26 June 1986), says that the past operating in Trevor's fiction is "more than merely personal or familial" (p. 32), and compares Trevor's writing in this regard to that of Pritchett, Faulkner, and Peter Taylor.

18 *Lovers of Their Time and Other Stories* (London: Bodley Head, 1978), p. 35. All quotations are from this edition.

19 At least one reviewer has argued that Cynthia's monologue near the end of the story is ineffective. In a review of *The Stories of William Trevor* and *Fools of Fortune*, *The Nation*, (3 Dec. 1983), Bernard McCabe says: "Clearly Trevor wants to link, in intensifying ways, the moral and psychological violence that this group visits upon itself to the larger horrors of Irish-English politics, where comparable malignities and victimizations prevail. But the revelation scene has too much work to do and seems stiff and strained" (pp. 575–6).

NOTES

20 John Fowles, in "The Irish Maupassant," a review of *The News from Ireland*, *The Atlantic*, (August 1986), sees this story in bleaker, more deterministic terms, saying that in it "a kind of malevolent, drifting determinism pervades human beings who cannot, or do not want to, cope" (p. 90).
21 Trevor has published a short story that contains the outlines of the plots and characters of *Fools of Fortune*. The story, entitled "Saints," was published in *The Atlantic Monthly*, (January 1981), pp. 29–36, but has not been reprinted in any of Trevor's collections of short stories.
22 *The Silence in the Garden* (London: Bodley Head, 1988), p. 183. All quotations are from this edition.
23 Patricia Craig, "The Shape of Past Iniquities," review of *The Silence in the Garden*, *The Times Literary Supplement*, (10–16 June 1988), p. 643.
24 "Remorse for Intemperate Speech," *The Collected Poems of W. B. Yeats* (New York: Macmillan, 1933, 1950, 1956), p. 249.

INDEX